THE POETS' YEAR

The Poets' Year

AN ANTHOLOGY

COMPILED BY

ADA SHARPLEY

CAMBRIDGE
AT THE UNIVERSITY PRESS
1922

TO

S. T. S.

CAMBRIDGE
UNIVERSITY PRESS

University Printing House, Cambridge CB2 8BS, United Kingdom

Cambridge University Press is part of the University of Cambridge.

It furthers the University's mission by disseminating knowledge in the pursuit of education, learning and research at the highest international levels of excellence.

www.cambridge.org
Information on this title: www.cambridge.org/9781107486744

© Cambridge University Press 1922

First published 1922
First paperback edition 2015

A catalogue record for this publication is available from the British Library

ISBN 978-1-107-48674-4 Paperback

PREFACE

THE days of the year have provided a framework for this anthology, but the care of the compiler has been not so much to fit each day with its poem as to place those chosen in the season to which they seem naturally to belong and in such sequence as to form a harmonious whole. For, as our lives must fit in with the course of the year, so also the poet's thoughts of life and death and beauty, and of the world seen as he only can see it, may find their setting in the seasons and in turn recreate them for us:

'He maketh his own sunrise, while he sings,
And turns the dusty world to Paradise.'

I owe thanks to many who have kindly allowed me to make use of copyright poems: to Mr John Murray for two poems by the Poet Laureate; to Mr Hilaire Belloc for a poem and to Messrs Duckworth and Co. for confirming the permission; to the late Wilfrid Scawen Blunt for a poem; to Messrs Heffer and Sons for a poem by Francis Békassy published in *Cambridge Poets, 1900–1913, an Anthology*; to Mr Laurence Binyon for two poems from *The Four Years* published by Mr Elkin Mathew who confirms the permission, and to the Editor of *The Times* for leave to reprint one of these poems; to the Literary Executor of Rupert Brooke and to Messrs Sidgwick and Jackson for two poems from 1914 *and Other Poems* by Rupert Brooke;

to Mrs Frances Cornford for several poems; to Messrs George Allen and Unwin for two poems by W. J. Cory from *Ionica*; to Mr Jonathan Cape for three poems by Mr W. H. Davies from *Nature Poems and Others*; to Mr Walter de la Mare for two poems; to Messrs Kegan Paul, Trench, Trübner and Co. for a poem by the late Mr Austin Dobson, and, together with the Rev. W. Miles Barnes, for several poems by William Barnes; to Mr John Drinkwater for a poem from *Swords and Ploughshares* published by Messrs Sidgwick and Jackson who confirm the permission; to Mr Philip Nutt for a poem by Mr Robert Frost and for one by Mr Walter Hogg; to Mr Thomas Hardy for two poems; to Messrs Macmillan and Co. for a poem by W. E. Henley and for one by Mr Ralph Hodgson; to Professor H. O. Meredith for a poem from *Week-Day Poems* published by Mr Edward Arnold who confirms the permission; to Messrs Chatto and Windus for two poems by Mr Robert Nichols and for one by R. L. Stevenson; to "Moira O'Neill" for a poem from *Songs of the Glens of Antrim*; to Mr Barry Pain for a poem; to Lord St Davids for a poem by the Hon. Colwyn Philipps; to Mr Ellis for a poem by D. G. Rossetti; to Mr T. Fisher Unwin for a poem by Miss M. McN. Sharpley which appeared in *The Independent Review*, and for one from the *Poems* of Mr W. B. Yeats published by him; to the Rev. E. Shillito for a poem from *The Omega and Other Poems* published by Mr B. H. Blackwell who confirms the permission; to Professor

Preface

Sorley for a poem by Charles Sorley from *Marlborough and Other Poems*; to Sir Herbert Stephen for two poems by J. K. Stephen; to Mr William Heinemann for a poem and two extracts by A. C. Swinburne from *Poems and Ballads*; to the Viscountess Grey for a poem by the Hon. Edward Wyndham Tennant; to Mrs Julius Tennyson and Mr W. C. A. Ker for a poem by Frederick Tennyson; to Mrs Edward Thomas for two poems by Edward Thomas; to Mr John Lane for part of a poem by Sir William Watson; to Major Francis Brett Young for a poem. The late Dr Todhunter kindly gave me permission for one of his poems and the late Mr Bertram Dobell for one by Thomas Traherne. My grateful thanks are due to the Oxford University Press for having kindly allowed me to make use of many of their texts.

A. S.

CAMBRIDGE
October 1922

JANUARY

THEN came old *January*, wrapped well
In many weeds to keep the cold away;
Yet did he quake and quiver like to quell,
And blow his nayles to warme them if he may:
For, they were numbd with holding all the day
An hatchet keene, with which he felled wood,
And from the trees did lop the needlesse spray:
Upon an huge great Earth-pot steane he stood;
From whose wide mouth, there flowed forth the
Romane floud.

Spenser

1

HERE we bring new water from the well so clear,
For to worship God with, this happy New Year.
Sing levy dew, sing levy dew, the water and the wine,
With seven bright gold wires, and bugles that do shine.
Sing reign of fair maid with gold upon her toe,
Open you the West door, and turn the Old Year go;
Sing reign of fair maid with gold upon her chin,
Open you the East door and turn the New Year in.

Anon

2

Therefore all seasons shall be sweet to thee,
Whether the summer clothe the general earth
With greenness, or the redbreast sit and sing
Betwixt the tufts of snow on the bare branch
Of mossy apple-tree, while the nigh thatch
Smokes in the sun-thaw; whether the eve-drops fall
Heard only in the trances of the blast,
Or if the secret ministry of frost
Shall hang them up in silent icicles,
Quietly shining to the quiet Moon.

S. T. Coleridge

3

A naked house, a naked moor,
A shivering pool before the door,
A garden bare of flowers and fruit,
And poplars at the garden foot:
Such is the house that I live in,
Bleak without and bare within.

Yet shall your barren moor receive
The incomparable pomp of eve,
And the cold glories of the dawn
Behind your shivering trees be drawn;
And when the wind from place to place
Doth the unmoored cloud-galleons chase,
Your garden gloom and gleam again
With leaping sun, with glancing rain.
Here shall the wizard moon ascend
The heavens, in the crimson end
Of day's declining splendour; here
The army of the stars appear.
The neighbour hollows dry or wet
Spring shall with tender flowers beset;
And oft the morning muser see
Larks rising from the broomy lea,
And every fairy wheel and thread
Of cobweb dew-bediamonded.
When daisies go shall winter-time
Silver the simple grass with rime;

January

Autumnal frosts enchant the pool
And make the cart-ruts beautiful;
And when snow-bright the moor expands,
How shall your children clap their hands!
To make this earth, our hermitage,
A cheerful and a changeful page,
God's bright and intricate device
Of days and seasons doth suffice.

R. L. Stevenson

4

Of this fair volume which we World do name,
If we the sheets and leaves could turn with care,
Of him who it corrects, and did it frame,
We clear might read the art and wisdom rare,
Find out his power which wildest powers doth tame,
His providence extending everywhere,
His justice, which proud rebels doth not spare,
In every page, no period of the same.
But silly we, like foolish children, rest
Well pleased with colour'd vellum, leaves of gold,
Fair dangling ribbands, leaving what is best,
On the great Writer's sense ne'er taking hold;
   Or if by chance we stay our minds on aught,
   It is some picture on the margin wrought.

William Drummond

5

How like an Angel came I down!
How bright are all things here!
When first among His works I did appear
O how their Glory me did crown!
The world resembled His Eternity,
In which my soul did walk;
And every thing that I did see
Did with me talk.

The skies in their magnificence,
The lively lovely air;
Oh how divine, how soft, how sweet, how fair!
The stars did entertain my sense,
And all the works of God, so bright and pure,
So rich and great did seem,
As if they ever must endure
In my esteem.

A native health and innocence
Within my bones did grow,
And while my God did all his Glories show,
I felt a vigour in my sense
That was all Spirit, I within did flow
With seas of life, like wine;
I nothing in the world did know
But 'twas divine.

Thomas Traherne

6

Fair, shining *Mountains* of my pilgrimage,
  And flow'ry *Vales*, whose flow'rs were stars:
The *days* and *nights* of my first, happy age;
  An age without distast and warrs:
When I by thoughts ascend your *Sunny heads*,
  And mind those sacred, *midnight* Lights:
By which I walk'd, when curtain'd Rooms and Beds
    Confin'd, or seal'd up others sights:
        O then how bright
        And quick a light
    Doth brush my heart and scatter night;
        Chasing that shade
        Which my sins made
    While I so *spring*, as if I could not *fade!*

How brave a prospect is a bright *Back-side!*
  Where flow'rs and palms refresh the Eye:
And days well spent like the glad *East* abide,
  Whose morning-glories cannot dye!

Henry Vaughan

7

And in the frosty season, when the sun
Was set, and visible for many a mile
The cottage windows blazed through twilight gloom,
I heeded not their summons: happy time
It was indeed for all of us—for me
It was a time of rapture! Clear and loud

The village clock tolled six,—I wheeled about,
Proud and exulting like an untired horse
That cares not for his home. All shod with steel,
We hissed along the polished ice in games
Confederate, imitative of the chase
And woodland pleasures,—the resounding horn,
The pack loud chiming, and the hunted hare.
So through the darkness and the cold we flew,
And not a voice was idle; with the din
Smitten, the precipices rang aloud;
The leafless trees and every icy crag
Tinkled like iron; while far distant hills
Into the tumult sent an alien sound
Of melancholy not unnoticed, while the stars
Eastward were sparkling clear, and in the west
The orange sky of evening died away.

Wordsworth

8

Robin on a leafless bough,
    Lord in Heaven, how he sings!
Now cold Winter's cruel wind
    Makes playmates of poor, dead things.

How he sings for joy this morn!
    How his breast doth pant and glow!
Look you how he stands and sings,
    Half-way up his legs in snow!

If these crumbs of bread were pearls,
And I had no bread at home,
He should have them for that song;
Pretty Robin Redbreast, Come.

W. H. Davies

9

Around the house the flakes fly faster,
And all the berries now are gone
From holly and cotoneaster
Around the house. The flakes fly! faster
Shutting indoors that crumb-outcaster
We used to see upon the lawn
Around the house. The flakes fly faster,
And all the berries now are gone!

Thomas Hardy

10

Snatched in short eddies, plays the withered leaf;
And on the flood the dancing feather floats.
With broadened nostrils to the sky upturned,
The conscious heifer snuffs the stormy gale.
Even, as the matron, at her nightly task,
With pensive labour draws the flaxen thread,
The wasted taper and the crackling flame
Foretell the blast. But chief the plumy race,
The tenants of the sky, its changes speak.
Retiring from the downs, where all day long

They picked their scanty fare, a blackening train
Of clamorous rooks thick-urge their weary flight,
And seek the closing shelter of the grove.
Assiduous, in his bower, the wailing owl
Plies his sad song. The cormorant on high
Wheels from the deep, and screams along the land.
Loud shrieks the soaring hern; and with wild wing
The circling sea-fowl cleave the flaky clouds.

James Thomson

II

Whither, midst falling dew,
While glow the heavens with the last steps of day,
Far, through their rosy depths, dost thou pursue
Thy solitary way?

Vainly the fowler's eye
Might mark thy distant flight to do thee wrong,
As, darkly painted on the crimson sky,
Thy figure floats along.

Seek'st thou the plashy brink
Of weedy lake, or marge of river wide,
Or where the rocking billows rise and sink
On the chafed ocean-side

There is a Power whose care
Teaches thy way along that pathless coast—
The desert and illimitable air—
Lone-wandering, but not lost.

All day thy wings have fanned,
At that far height, the cold thin atmosphere,
Yet stoop not, weary, to the welcome land,
   Though the dark night is near.

And soon that toil shall end,
Soon shalt thou find a summer home, and rest
And scream among thy fellows; reeds shall bend
   Soon o'er thy sheltered nest.

Thou art gone—the abyss of heaven
Hath swallowed up thy form; yet on my heart
Deeply hath sunk the lesson thou hast given,
   And shall not soon depart.

He who, from zone to zone,
Guides through the boundless sky thy certain flight,
In the long way that I must tread alone,
   Will lead my steps aright.

               W. C. Bryant

12

I saw faire Chloris walke alone,
When feather'd raine came softly down,
Then Jove descended from his tower
To court her in a silver shower,
The wanton snow flew to her brest,
Like little birds into their nest;

But overcome with whiteness there,
For griefe it thaw'd into a teare,
Then falling down her garment hem,
To decke her, froze into a gem.

Anon

13

When icicles hang by the wall,
  And Dick the shepherd blows his nail,
And Tom bears logs into the hall,
  And milk comes frozen home in pail,
When blood is nipp'd and ways be foul,
Then nightly sings the staring owl,
     To-whit!
To-who!—a merry note,
While greasy Joan doth keel the pot.

When all aloud the wind doth blow,
  And coughing drowns the parson's saw,
And birds sit brooding in the snow,
  And Marian's nose looks red and raw,
When roasted crabs hiss in the bowl,
Then nightly sings the staring owl,
     To-whit!
To-who!—a merry note,
While greasy Joan doth keel the pot.

Shakespeare

14

The days are cold, the nights are long,
The north-wind sings a doleful song;
Then hush again upon my breast;
All merry things are now at rest,
  Save thee, my pretty Love!

The kitten sleeps upon the hearth,
The crickets long have ceased their mirth;
There's nothing stirring in the house
Save one wee, hungry, nibbling mouse,
  Then why so busy thou?

Nay! start not at that sparkling light;
'Tis but the moon that shines so bright
On the window pane bedropped with rain:
Then little Darling! sleep again,
  And wake when it is day.

Wordsworth

15

'I have no name:
I am but two days old.'
What shall I call thee?
'I happy am,
Joy is my name.'
Sweet joy befall thee!

Pretty Joy!
Sweet Joy, but two days old.
Sweet Joy I call thee:
Thou dost smile,
I sing the while,
Sweet joy befall thee!

William Blake

16

Edmund Spenser died January 16, 1599.

Rapt with the rage of mine own ravisht thought,
　Through contemplation of those goodly sights,
　And glorious images in heaven wrought,
　Whose wondrous beauty breathing sweet delights,
　Do kindle love in high conceipted sprights:
　I faine to tell the things that I behold,
But feele my wits to faile, and tongue to fold.

Vouchsafe then, O thou most almightie Spright,
　From whom all guifts of wit and knowledge flow,
　To shed into my breast some sparkling light
　Of thine eternall Truth, that I may show
　Some little beames to mortall eyes below,
　Of that immortall beautie, there with thee,
Which in my weake distraughted mynd I see.

That with the glorie of so goodly sight,
　The hearts of men, which fondly here admyre
　Faire seeming shewes, and feed on vaine delight,
　Transported with celestiall desyre

Of those faire formes, may lift themselves up hyer,
And learne to love with zealous humble dewty,
Th'eternall fountaine of that heavenly beauty.

Spenser

17

If music and sweet poetry agree,
As they must needs, the sister and the brother,
Then must the love be great 'twixt thee and me,
Because thou lov'st the one, and I the other.
Dowland to thee is dear, whose heavenly touch
Upon the lute doth ravish human sense;
Spenser to me, whose deep conceit is such,
As, passing all conceit, needs no defence.
Thou lov'st to hear the sweet melodious sound
That Phoebus' lute, the queen of music, makes;
And I in deep delight am chiefly drown'd
Whenas himself to singing he betakes.
  One god is god of both, as poets feign;
  One knight loves both, and both in thee remain.

Richard Barnefield

18

For deeds doe die, how ever noblie donne,
And thoughts of men do as themselves decay,
But wise wordes, taught in numbers for to runne,
Recorded by the Muses, live for ay;

Ne may with storming showers be washt away,
Ne bitter breathing windes with harmfull blast,
Nor age, nor envie, shall them ever wast.

But fame with golden wings aloft doth flie,
Above the reach of ruinous decay,
And with brave plumes doth beate the azure skie,
Admir'd of base-borne men from farre away:
Then, who so will with vertuous deeds assay
To mount to heaven, on *Pegasus* must ride,
And with sweete Poets verse be glorifide.

Spenser

19

Like as the waves make towards the pebbled shore,
So do our minutes hasten to their end;
Each changing place with that which goes before,
In sequent toil all forwards do contend.
Nativity, once in the main of light,
Crawls to maturity, wherewith being crown'd,
Crooked eclipses 'gainst his glory fight,
And Time that gave doth now his gift confound.
Time doth transfix the flourish set on youth
And delves the parallels in beauty's brow,
Feeds on the rarities of nature's truth,
And nothing stands but for his scythe to mow:
    And yet to times in hope my verse shall stand,
    Praising thy worth, despite his cruel hand.

Shakespeare

20

I dreamed that, as I wandered by the way,
  Bare Winter suddenly was changed to Spring,
And gentle odours led my steps astray,
  Mixed with a sound of waters murmuring
Along a shelving bank of turf, which lay
  Under a copse, and hardly dared to fling
Its green arms round the bosom of the stream,
But kissed it and then fled, as thou mightest in dream.

There grew pied wind-flowers and violets,
  Daisies, those pearled Arcturi of the earth,
The constellated flower that never sets;
  Faint oxslips; tender blue bells, at whose birth
The sod scarce heaved; and that tall flower that wets—
  Like a child, half in tenderness and mirth—
Its mother's face with Heaven's collected tears,
When the low wind, its playmate's voice, it hears.

And in the warm hedge grew lush eglantine,
  Green cowbind and the moonlight-colour'd may,
And cherry-blossoms, and white cups, whose wine
  Was the bright dew, yet drain'd not by the day;
And wild roses, and ivy serpentine,
  With its dark buds and leaves, wandering astray;
And flowers azure, black, and streaked with gold,
Fairer than any wakened eyes behold.

And nearer to the river's trembling edge
  There grew broad flag-flowers, purple pranked
    with white,
And starry river buds among the sedge,
  And floating water-lilies, broad and bright,
Which lit the oak that overhung the hedge
  With moonlight beams of their own watery light;
And bulrushes, and reeds of such deep green
As soothed the dazzled eye with sober sheen.

Methought that of these visionary flowers
  I made a nosegay, bound in such a way
That the same hues, which in their natural bowers
  Were mingled or opposed, the like array
Kept these imprisoned children of the Hours
  Within my hand,—and then, elate and gay,
I hastened to the spot whence I had come,
That I might there present it!—Oh! to whom?

Shelley

21

Fancy, high-commission'd:—send her!
She has vassals to attend her:
She will bring, in spite of frost,
Beauties that the earth hath lost;
She will bring thee, all together,
All delights of summer weather;
All the buds and bells of May,
From dewy sward or thorny spray;

All the heapèd Autumn's wealth,
With a still, mysterious stealth:
She will mix these pleasures up
Like three fit wines in a cup,
And thou shalt quaff it:—thou shalt hear
Distant harvest-carols clear;
Rustle of the reapèd corn;
Sweet birds antheming the morn:
And, in the same moment—hark!
'Tis the early April lark,
Or the rooks, with busy caw,
Foraging for sticks and straw.
Thou shalt, at one glance, behold
The daisy and the marigold;
White-plum'd lillies, and the first
Hedge-grown primrose that hath burst;
Shaded hyacinth, alway
Sapphire queen of the mid-May;
And every leaf, and every flower
Pearlèd with the self-same shower.

Keats

22

O Proserpina!
For the flowers now that frighted thou let'st fall
From Dis's waggon! daffodils,
That come before the swallow dares, and take
The winds of March with beauty; violets dim,
But sweeter than the lids of Juno's eyes

Or Cytherea's breath; pale prime-roses,
That die unmarried, ere they can behold
Bright Phoebus in his strength, a malady
Most incident to maids; bold oxlips and
The crown imperial; lilies of all kinds,
The flower-de-luce being one.

Shakespeare

23

The poetry of earth is never dead:
  When all the birds are faint with the hot sun,
  And hide in cooling trees, a voice will run
From hedge to hedge about the new-mown mead;
That is the Grasshopper's—he takes the lead
  In summer luxury,—he has never done
  With his delights; for when tired out with fun
He rests at ease beneath some pleasant weed.
The poetry of earth is ceasing never:
  On a lone winter evening, when the frost
    Has wrought a silence, from the stove there shrills
The Cricket's song, in warmth increasing ever,
  And seems to one in drowsiness half lost,
    The Grasshopper's among some grassy hills.

Keats

24

Far, far, from here,
The Adriatic breaks in a warm bay
Among the green Illyrian hills; and there
The sunshine in the happy glens is fair,

2—2

And by the sea, and in the brakes.
The grass is cool, the sea-side air
Buoyant and fresh, the mountain flowers
More virginal and sweet than ours.
And there, they say, two bright and aged snakes,
Who once were Cadmus and Harmonia,
Bask in the glens or on the warm sea-shore,
In breathless quiet, after all their ills.
Nor do they see their country, nor the place
Where the Sphinx lived among the frowning hills,
Nor the unhappy palace of their race,
Nor Thebes, nor the Ismenus, any more.

There those two live, far in the Illyrian brakes.
They had stay'd long enough to see,
In Thebes, the billow of calamity
Over their own dear children roll'd,
Curse upon curse, pang upon pang,
For years, they sitting helpless in their home,
A grey old man and woman; yet of old
The Gods had to their marriage come,
And at the banquet all the Muses sang.

Therefore they did not end their days
In sight of blood; but were rapt, far away,
To where the west wind plays,
And murmurs of the Adriatic come
To those untrodden mountain lawns; and there
Placed safely in changed forms, the Pair

Wholly forget their first sad life, and home,
And all that Theban woe, and stray
For ever through the glens, placid and dumb.

Matthew Arnold

25

Orpheus with his lute made trees,
And the mountain tops that freeze,
  Bow themselves, when he did sing:
To his music plants and flowers
Ever sprung; as sun and showers
  There had made a lasting spring.

Every thing that heard him play,
Even the billows of the sea,
  Hung their heads, and then lay by.
In sweet music is such art,
  Killing care and grief of heart
  Fall asleep, or hearing, die.

Shakespeare

26

When Orpheus sweetly did complain
Upon his Lute with heavy strain,
How his Eurydice was slain;
    The Trees to hear
    Obtain'd an Ear
And after left it off again.

At every stroke, and every stay,
The Boughs kept time, and nodding lay,
And listned bending every way;
  The Ashen-Tree
  As well as he
Began to shake, and learnt to play.

If Wood could speak, a Tree might hear,
If Wood can sound our Grief so near,
A Tree might drop an amber Tear:
  If Wood so well
  Could sound a Knell,
The Cypress might condole the bier.

The standing Nobles of the Grove,
Hearing dead Wood to speak and move,
The fatal Ax began to love;
  They envied Death
  That gave such breath,
As Men alive do Saints above.

         Anon

27

Ariel to Miranda:—Take
This slave of Music, for the sake
Of him, who is the slave of thee,
And teach it all the harmony
In which thou canst, and only thou,
Make the delighted spirit glow,
Till joy denies itself again,

And, too intense, is turned to pain;
For by permission and command
Of thine own Prince Ferdinand,
Poor Ariel sends this silent token
Of more than ever can be spoken;
Your guardian spirit, Ariel, who,
From life to life, must still pursue
Your happiness;—for thus alone
Can Ariel ever find his own.
From Prospero's enchanted cell,
As the mighty verses tell,
To the throne of Naples, he
Lit you o'er the trackless sea,
Flitting on, your prow before,
Like a living meteor.
When you die, the silent Moon,
In her interlunar swoon,
Is not sadder in her cell
Than deserted Ariel.
When you live again on earth,
Like an unseen star of birth,
Ariel guides you o'er the sea
Of life from your nativity.
Many changes have been run
Since Ferdinand and you begun
Your course of love, and Ariel still
Has tracked your steps, and served your will;
Now, in humbler, happier lot,
This is all remembered not;

And now, alas! the poor sprite is
Imprisoned, for some fault of his,
In a body like a grave;
From you he only dares to crave,
For his service and his sorrow,
A smile to-day, a song to-morrow.

The artist who this idol wrought,
To echo all harmonious thought,
Felled a tree, while on the steep
The woods were in their winter sleep,
Rocked in that repose divine
On the wind-swept Apennine;
And dreaming, some of Autumn past,
And some of Spring approaching fast,
And some of April buds and showers,
And some of songs in July bowers,
And all of love; and so this tree,—
O that such our death may be!—
Died in sleep, and felt no pain,
To live in happier form again:
From which, beneath Heaven's fairest star,
The artist wrought this loved Guitar,
And taught it justly to reply,
To all who question skilfully,
In language gentle as thine own;
Whispering in enamoured tone
Sweet oracles of woods and dells,
And summer winds in sylvan cells;

For it had learned all harmonies
Of the plains and of the skies,
Of the forests and the mountains,
And the many-voicèd fountains;
The clearest echoes of the hills,
The softest notes of falling rills,
The melodies of birds and bees,
The murmuring of summer seas,
And pattering rain, and breathing dew,
And airs of evening; and it knew
That seldom-heard mysterious sound,
Which, driven on its diurnal round,
As it floats through boundless day,
Our world enkindles on its way.—
All this it knows, but will not tell
To those who cannot question well
The Spirit that inhabits it;
It talks according to the wit
Of its companions; and no more
Is heard than has been felt before,
By those who tempt it to betray
These secrets of an elder day:
But, sweetly as its answers will
Flatter hands of perfect skill,
It keeps its highest, holiest tone
For our beloved Jane alone.

Shelley

28

Charm me asleep, and melt me so
 With thy Delicious Numbers;
That being ravisht, hence I goe
 Away in easie slumbers.
 Ease my sick head,
 And make my bed,
 Thou Power that canst sever
 From me this ill:
 And quickly still:
 Though thou not kill
 My Fever.

Thou sweetly canst convert the same
 From a consuming fire,
Into a gentle-licking flame,
 And make it thus expire.
 Then make me weep
 My paines asleep;
 And give me such reposes,
 That I, poore I,
 May think, thereby,
 I live and die
 'Mongst Roses.

Fall on me like a silent dew,
 Or like those Maiden showrs,
Which, by the peepe of day, doe strew
 A baptime o're the flowers.

Melt, melt my paines,
With thy soft straines;
That having ease me given,
With full delight,
I leave this light;
And take my flight
For Heaven.

Robert Herrick

29

Lone Flower, hemmed in with snows, and white as they,
But hardier far, once more I see thee bend
Thy forehead as if fearful to offend,
Like an unbidden guest. Though day by day
Storms, sallying from the mountain-tops, waylay
The rising sun, and on the plains descend;
Yet art thou welcome, welcome as a friend
Whose zeal outruns his promise! Blue-eyed May
Shall soon behold this border thickly set
With bright jonquils, their odours lavishing
On the soft west-wind and his frolic peers;
Nor will I then thy modest grace forget,
Chaste Snowdrop, venturous harbinger of Spring,
And pensive monitor of fleeting years!

Wordsworth

30

He nothing common did, or mean,
Upon that memorable scene;
   But with his keener eye
   The axe's edge did try;
Nor call'd the gods, with vulgar spight,
To vindicate his helplesse right:
   But bow'd his comely head
   Downe, as upon a bed.

Andrew Marvell

31

The glories of our blood and state
   Are shadows, not substantial things;
There is no armour against fate;
   Death lays his icy hand on kings:
     Sceptre and Crown
     Must tumble down,
And in the dust be equal made
With the poor crooked scythe and spade.

Some men with swords may reap the field,
   And plant fresh laurels where they kill:
But their strong nerves at last must yield;
   They tame but one another still:
     Early or late
     They stoop to fate,
And must give up their murmuring breath
When they, pale captives, creep to death.

The garlands wither on your brow;
  Then boast no more your mighty deeds;
Upon Death's purple altar now
  See where the victor-victim bleeds:
      Your heads must come
      To the cold tomb;
Only the actions of the just
Smell sweet, and blossom in their dust.

James Shirley

FEBRUARY

And lastly, came cold *February*, sitting
  In an old wagon, for he could not ride;
  Drawne of two fishes for the season fitting,
  Which through the flood before did softly slyde
  And swim away: yet had he by his side
  His plough and harnesse fit to till the ground,
  And tooles to prune the trees, before the pride
  Of hasting Prime did make them burgein round:
So past the twelve Months forth, and their dew places
     found.

Spenser

I

Down with the Rosemary and Bayes,
    Down with the Misleto;
In stead of Holly, now up-raise
    The greener Box (for show.)

The Holly hitherto did sway;
    Let Box now domineere;
Untill the dancing Easter-day,
    Or Easters Eve appeare.

Then youthfull Box which now hath grace,
    Your houses to renew;
Grown old, surrender must his place,
    Unto the crisped Yew.

When Yew is out, then Birch comes in,
    And many Flowers beside;
Both of a fresh, and fragrant kinne,
    To honour Whitsontide.

Green Rushes then, and sweetest Bents,
    With cooler Oken boughs;
Come in for comely ornaments,
    To re-adorn the house.

Thus times do shift; each thing his turne do's hold;
New things succeed, as former things grow old.
                   Robert Herrick

2

New doth the sun appear,
The mountains' snows decay,
Crown'd with frail flowers forth comes the baby
    year.
My soul, time posts away,
And thou yet in that frost
Which flower and fruit hath lost,
As if all here immortal were, dost stay:
For shame! thy powers awake,
Look to that heaven which never night makes
    black,
And there, at that immortal sun's bright rays,
Deck thee with flowers which fear not rage of
    days.

William Drummond

3

The weary yeare his race now having run,
    The new begins his compast course anew:
    With shew of morning mylde he hath begun,
    Betokening peace and plenty to ensew.
So let us, which this chaunge of weather vew,
    Chaunge eeke our mynds and former lives amend,
    The old yeares sinnes forepast let us eschew,
    And fly the faults with which we did offend.

Then shall the new yeares joy forth freshly send,
   Into the glooming world his gladsome ray:
   And all these stormes which now his beauty blend,
   Shall turne to caulmes and tymely cleare away.
So likewise love cheare you your heavy spright,
   And chaunge old yeares annoy to new delight.

Spenser

4

   The crocus, while the days are dark,
      Unfolds its saffron sheen;
   At April's touch, the crudest bark
      Discovers gems of green.

   Then sleep the seasons, full of might;
      While slowly swells the pod
   And rounds the peach, and in the night
      The mushroom bursts the sod.

   The Winter falls; the frozen rut
      Is bound with silver bars;
   The snow-drift heaps against the hut;
      And night is pierc'd with stars.

Coventry Patmore

5

Mysterious Night! when our first parent knew
Thee from report divine, and heard thy name,
Did he not tremble for this lovely frame,
This glorious canopy of light and blue?

Yet 'neath a curtain of translucent dew,
Bathed in the rays of the great setting flame,
Hesperus with the host of heaven came,
And lo! creation widened in man's view.
Who could have thought such darkness lay concealed
Within thy beams, O sun! or who could find,
Whilst fly, and leaf, and insect stood revealed,
That to such countless orbs thou mad'st us blind!
Why do we then shun death with anxious strife?
If light can thus deceive, wherefore not life?

Blanco White

6

Fair, order'd lights, (whose motion without noise
   Resembles those true Joys
Whose spring is on that hil where you do grow
   And we here tast sometimes below,)

With what exact obedience do you move
   Now beneath, and now above,
And in your vast progressions overlook
   The darkest night, and closest nook!

Some nights I see you in the gladsome East,
   Some others neer the West,
And when I cannot see, yet do you shine,
   And beat about your endles line.

Silence, and light, and watchfulnes with you
    Attend and wind the Clue,
No sleep, nor sloth assailes you, but poor man
    Still either sleeps, or slips his span.

He grops beneath here, and with restless Care
    First makes, then hugs a snare,
Adores dead dust, sets heart on Corne and grass
    But seldom doth make heav'n his glass.

Musick and mirth (if there be musick here)
    Take up, and tune his year,
These things are Kin to him and must be had,
    Who kneels, or sighs a life is mad.

Perhaps some nights hee'l watch with you and peep
    When it were best to sleep,
Dares know Effects, and Judge them long before,
    When th' herb he treads knows much, much more.

But seeks he your *Obedience, Order, Light,*
    Your calm and wel-train'd flight,
Where, though the glory differ in each star,
    Yet is there peace still, and no war.

                        Henry Vaughan

7

Wide are the meadows of night,
And daisies are shining there,
Tossing their lovely dews,
Lustrous and fair;

And through these sweet fields go,
Wanderers amid the stars—
Venus, Mercury, Uranus, Neptune,
Saturn, Jupiter, Mars.

'Tired in their silver, they move,
And circling, whisper and say,
Fair are the blossoming meads of delight
Through which we stray.

Walter de la Mare

8

Set where the upper streams of Simois flow
Was the Palladium, high 'mid rock and wood;
And Hector was in Ilium, far below,
And fought, and saw it not, but there it stood.

It stood; and sun and moonshine rain'd their light
On the pure columns of its glen-built hall.
Backward and forward roll'd the waves of fight
Round Troy; but while this stood, Troy could not fall.

So, in its lovely moonlight, lives the soul.
Mountains surround it, and sweet virgin air;
Cold plashing, past it, crystal waters roll;
We visit it by moments, ah! too rare.

Men will renew the battle in the plain
To-morrow; red with blood will Xanthus be;
Hector and Ajax will be there again;
Helen will come upon the wall to see.

Then we shall rust in shade, or shine in strife,
And fluctuate 'twixt blind hopes and blind despairs,
And fancy that we put forth all our life,
And never know how with the soul it fares.

Still doth the soul, from its lone fastness high,
Upon our life a ruling effluence send;
And when it fails, fight as we will, we die;
And while it lasts, we cannot wholly end.

Matthew Arnold

9

O! it is pleasant, with a heart at ease,
  Just after sunset, or by moonlight skies,
To make the shifting clouds be what you please,
  Or let the easily persuaded eyes
Own each quaint likeness issuing from the mould
  Of a friend's fancy; or with head bent low
And cheek aslant see rivers flow of gold
  'Twixt crimson banks; and then a traveller, go
From mount to mount through Cloudland, gorgeous
      land!
  Or list'ning to the tide, with closed sight,
Be that blind bard, who on the Chian strand
  By those deep sounds possessed with inward light,
Beheld the Iliad and the Odyssee
  Rise to the swelling of the voiceful sea.

S. T. Coleridge

10

Piping down the valleys wild,
Piping songs of pleasant glee,
On a cloud I saw a child,
And he laughing said to me:

'Pipe a song about a Lamb!'
So I piped with merry cheer.
'Piper, pipe that song again;'
So I piped: he wept to hear.

'Drop thy pipe, thy happy pipe;
Sing thy songs of happy cheer:'
So I sang the same again,
While he wept with joy to hear.

'Piper, sit thee down and write
In a book, that all may read.'
So he vanish'd from my sight,
And I pluck'd a hollow reed,

And I made a rural pen,
And I stain'd the water clear,
And I wrote my happy songs
Every child may joy to hear.

William Blake

11

Little Lamb, who made thee?
Dost thou know who made thee?
Gave thee life, and bid thee feed,
By the stream and o'er the mead;
Gave thee clothing of delight,
Softest clothing, woolly, bright;
Gave thee such a tender voice,
Making all the vales rejoice?
Little Lamb, who made thee?
Dost thou know who made thee?

Little Lamb, I'll tell thee,
Little Lamb, I'll tell thee:
He is callèd by thy name,
For He calls Himself a Lamb.
He is meek and He is mild;
He became a little child.
I a child, and thou a lamb,
We are callèd by His name.
Little Lamb, God bless thee!
Little Lamb, God bless thee!

William Blake

12

Tiger! tiger! burning bright
In the forests of the night,
What immortal hand or eye
Could frame thy fearful symmetry?

In what distant deeps or skies
Burnt the fire of thine eyes?
On what wings dare he aspire?
What the hand dare seize the fire?

And what shoulder, and what art,
Could twist the sinews of thy heart?
And when thy heart began to beat,
What dread hand? and what dread feet?

What the hammer? what the chain?
In what furnace was thy brain?
What the anvil? what dread grasp
Dare its deadly terrors clasp?

When the stars threw down their spears,
And water'd heaven with their tears,
Did he smile his work to see?
Did he who made the Lamb make thee?

Tiger! tiger! burning bright
In the forests of the night,
What immortal hand or eye
Dare frame thy fearful symmetry?

William Blake

13

Thou wilt remember one warm morn, when Winter
Crept aged from the earth, and Spring's first breath
Blew soft from the moist hills; the black-thorn boughs,
So dark in the bare wood, when glistening
In the sunshine were white with coming buds,
Like the bright side of a sorrow, and the banks
Had violets opening from sleep like eyes.

Robert Browning

14

Now welcom somer, with thy sonne softe,
That hast this wintres weders over-shake,
And driven awey the longe nightes blake!

Seynt Valentyn, that art ful hy on-lofte;—
Thus singen smale foules for thy sake—
 Now welcom somer, with thy sonne softe,
 That hast this wintres weders over-shake.

Wel han they cause for to gladen ofte,
Sith ech of hem recovered hath his make;
Ful blisful may they singen whan they wake;
 Now welcom somer, with thy sonne softe,
 That hast this wintres weders over-shake,
 And driven awey the longe nightes blake.

Chaucer

15

To-day, all day, I rode upon the down,
With hounds and horsemen, a brave company.
On this side in its glory lay the sea,
On that the Sussex weald, a sea of brown.
The wind was light, and brightly the sun shone,
And still we gallop'd on from gorse to gorse:
And once, when check'd, a thrush sang, and my horse
Prick'd his quick ears as to a sound unknown.
    I knew the Spring was come. I knew it even
Better than all by this, that through my chase
In bush and stone and hill and sea and heaven
I seem'd to see and follow still your face.
Your face my quarry was. For it I rode,
My horse a thing of wings, myself a god.

                Wilfred Scawen Blunt

16

High-way, since you my chief *Parnassus* be,
And that my muse, to some ears not unsweet,
Tempers her words to trampling horse's feet,
    More oft than to a chamber melody,
Now blessed you, bear onward blessed me
    To her, where I my heart safe-left, shall meet;
    My muse and I must you of duty greet,

February

With thanks and wishes, wishing thankfully,
　　Be you still fair, honour'd by publick heed;
By no encroachment wrong'd, nor time forgot:
　　Nor blam'd for blood, nor sham'd for sinful deed;
And that you know, I envy you no lot
　　Of highest wish, I wish you so much bliss,
　　Hundreds of years you *Stella's* feet may kiss.

Sir Philip Sidney

17

Were I as base as is the lowly plain,
And you, my Love, as high as heaven above,
Yet should the thoughts of me your humble swain
Ascend to heaven, in honour of my Love.
Were I as high as heaven above the plain,
And you, my Love, as humble and as low
As are the deepest bottoms of the main,
Whereso'er you were, with you my love should go.
Were you the earth, dear Love, and I the skies,
My love should shine on you like to the sun,
And look upon you with ten thousand eyes
Till heaven wax'd blind, and till the world were done.
Whereso'er I am, below, or else above you,
Whereso'er you are, my heart shall truly love you.

Joshua Sylvester

18

At the corner of Wood Street, when daylight appears,
Hangs a Thrush that sings loud, it has sung for three
    years:
Poor Susan has passed by the spot, and has heard
In the silence of morning the song of the Bird.

'Tis a note of enchantment; what ails her? She sees
A mountain ascending, a vision of trees;
Bright volumes of vapour through Lothbury glide,
And a river flows on through the vale of Cheapside.

Green pastures she views in the midst of the dale,
Down which she so often has tripped with her pail;
And a single small cottage, a nest like a dove's,
The one only dwelling on earth that she loves.

She looks, and her heart is in heaven: but they fade,
The mist and the river, the hill and the shade:
The stream will not flow, and the hill will not rise,
And the colours have all passed away from her eyes!

Wordsworth

19

A child in the city,
So solemn and wise,
With dirt on its fingers,
And dust in its eyes.

February

If I were a gipsy,
With long brown arms,
I would hug it, and steal it
Away from all harms.

And in the green lane
Where my gipsy-tent stands,
It should lie in my arms
And feed from my hands.

It should drink of sweet milk
And wash in the streams,
Whose voices all night
Should sound through its dreams.

It should know the wild creatures
And herbs as they grow,
The stars how they shine,
The winds how they blow,

The sun in the morning,
The grass in the rain,
And never return
To the city again.

Frances Cornford

20

Who can live in heart so glad
As the merry country lad?
Who upon a fair green balk
May at pleasure sit and walk,

And amid the azure skies
See the morning sun arise,—
While he hears in every spring
How the birds do chirp and sing:
Or before the hounds in cry
See the hare go stealing by:
Or along the shallow brook,
Angling with a baited hook,
See the fishes leap and play
In a blessèd sunny day:
Or to hear the partridge call,
Till she have her covey all:
Or to see the subtle fox,
How the villain plies the box;
After feeding on his prey,
How he closely sneaks away,
Through the hedge and down the furrow
Till he gets into his burrow;
Then the bee to gather honey,
And the little black-haired coney,
On a bank for sunny place,
With her forefeet wash her face:
Are not these, with thousands moe
Than the courts of kings do know,
The true pleasing spirit's sights
That may breed true love's delights?

Nicholas Breton

21

Where the pools are bright and deep,
Where the grey trout lies asleep,
Up the river and over the lea,
That's the way for Billy and me.

Where the blackbird sings the latest,
Where the hawthorn blooms the sweetest,
Where the nestlings chirp and flee,
That's the way for Billy and me.

Where the mowers mow the cleanest,
Where the hay lies thick and greenest,
There to track the homeward bee,
That's the way for Billy and me.

Where the hazel bank is steepest,
Where the shadow falls the deepest,
Where the clustering nuts fall free,
That's the way for Billy and me.

Why the boys should drive away
Little sweet maidens from the play,
Or love to banter and fight so well,
That's the thing I never could tell.

But this I know, I love to play
Through the meadow, among the hay;
Up the water and over the lea,
That's the way for Billy and me.

James Hogg

22

When the voices of children are heard on the green,
And laughing is heard on the hill,
My heart is at rest within my breast,
And everything else is still.

'Then come home, my children, the sun is gone down,
And the dews of night arise;
Come, come, leave off play, and let us away
Till the morning appears in the skies.'

'No, no, let us play, for it is yet day,
And we cannot go to sleep;
Besides, in the sky the little birds fly,
And the hills are all cover'd with sheep.'

'Well, well, go and play till the light fades away,
And then go home to bed.'
The little ones leaped and shouted and laugh'd
And all the hills echoèd.

William Blake

23

John Keats died February 23, 1821.

I weep for Adonais—he is dead!
O, weep for Adonais! though our tears
Thaw not the frost which binds so dear a head!
And thou, sad Hour, selected from all years

To mourn our loss, rouse thy obscure compeers,
And teach them thine own sorrow, say: 'With me
Died Adonais; till the Future dares
Forget the Past, his fate and fame shall be
An echo and a light unto eternity!'

Shelley

24

When I have fears that I may cease to be
Before my pen has glean'd my teeming brain,
Before high piled books, in charact'ry,
Hold like rich garners the full-ripen'd grain;
When I behold, upon the night's starr'd face,
Huge cloudy symbols of a high romance,
And feel that I may never live to trace
Their shadows, with the magic hand of chance;
And when I feel, fair creature of an hour!
That I shall never look upon thee more,
Never have relish in the faery power
Of unreflecting love!—then on the shore
Of the wide world I stand alone, and think
Till Love and Fame to nothingness do sink.

Keats

25

In my former days of bliss,
Her divine skill taught me this,
That from every thing I saw,
I could some invention draw;

And raise pleasure to her height,
Through the meanest object's sight;
By the murmur of a spring,
Or the least bough's rustling;
By a daisie, whose leaves spread,
Shut when Titan goes to bed;
Or a shady bush or tree;
She could more infuse in me,
Than all Nature's beauties can
In some other wiser man...
Poesy, thou sweet'st content
That e'er Heav'n to mortals lent!
Though they as a trifle leave thee,
Whose dull thoughts cannot conceive thee,
Though thou be to them a scorn,
That to nought but earth are born;
Let my life no longer be
Than I am in love with thee.

George Wither

26

Whether on Ida's shady brow,
Or in the chambers of the East,
The chambers of the sun, that now
From ancient melody have ceas'd;

Whether in Heaven ye wander fair,
Or the green corners of the earth,
Or the blue regions of the air
Where the melodious winds have birth;

February

Whether on crystal rocks ye rove,
Beneath the bosom of the sea
Wand'ring in many a coral grove,
Fair Nine, forsaking Poetry!

How have you left the ancient love
That bards of old enjoy'd in you!
The languid strings do scarcely move!
The sound is forc'd, the notes are few!

William Blake

27

Best and brightest, come away!
Fairer far than this fair Day,
Which, like thee to those in sorrow,
Comes to bid a sweet good-morrow
To the rough year just awake
In its cradle on the brake.
The brightest hour of unborn Spring,
Through the winter wandering,
Found, it seems, the halcyon Morn
To hoar February born.
Bending from Heaven, in azure mirth,
It kissed the forehead of the Earth,
And smiled upon the silent sea,
And bade the frozen streams be free,
And waked to music all their fountains,
And breathed upon the frozen mountains,

And like a prophetess of May
Strewed flowers upon the barren way,
Making the wintry world appear
Like one on whom thou smilest, dear.

Shelley

28

Then all is still; earth is a wintry clod:
But spring-wind, like a dancing psaltress, passes
Over its breast to waken it, rare verdure
Buds tenderly upon rough banks, between
The withered tree-roots and the cracks of frost,
Like a smile striving with a wrinkled face;
The grass grows bright, the boughs are swoln with
        blooms
Like chrysalids impatient for the air,
The shining dorrs are busy, beetles run
Along the furrows, ants make their ado;
Above, birds fly in merry flocks, the lark
Soars up and up, shivering for very joy;
Afar the ocean sleeps; white fishing-gulls
Flit where the strand is purple with its tribe
Of nested limpets; savage creatures seek
Their loves in wood and plain—and God renews
His ancient rapture.

Robert Browning

MARCH

THESE, marching softly, thus in order went,
    And after them, the Monthes all riding came;
    First, sturdy *March* with brows full sternly bent,
    And armed strongly, rode upon a Ram,
    The same which over *Hellespontus* swam:
    Yet in his hand a spade he also hent,
    And in a bag all sorts of seeds ysame,
    Which on the earth he strowed as he went,
And fild her womb with fruitfull hope of nourish-
        ment.

Spenser

March

I

It is the first mild day of March:
Each minute sweeter than before,
The redbreast sings from the tall larch
That stands beside our door.

There is a blessing in the air,
Which seems a sense of joy to yield
To the bare trees, and mountains bare,
And grass in the green field.

My sister! ('tis a wish of mine)
Now that our morning meal is done,
Make haste, your morning task resign;
Come forth and feel the sun.

Edward will come with you;—and, pray,
Put on with speed your woodland dress;
And bring no book: for this one day
We'll give to idleness.

No joyless forms shall regulate
Our living calendar:
We from to-day, my Friend, will date
The opening of the year.

Love, now a universal birth,
From heart to heart is stealing,
From earth to man, from man to earth:
—It is the hour of feeling.

March

One moment now may give us more
Than years of toiling reason:
Our minds shall drink at every pore
The spirit of the season.

Some silent laws our hearts will make,
Which they shall long obey:
We for the year to come may take
Our temper from to-day.

And from the blessed power that rolls
About, below, above,
We'll frame the measure of our souls:
They shall be tuned to love.

Then come, my Sister! come, I pray,
With speed put on your woodland dress;
And bring no book: for this one day
We'll give to idleness.

Wordsworth

2

Winters know
Easily to shed the snow,
And the untaught Spring is wise
In cowslips and anemones.
Nature, hating art and pains,
Baulks and baffles plotting brains;
Casualty and Surprise
Are the apples of her eyes;

But she dearly loves the poor,
And, by marvel of her own,
Strikes the loud pretender down.
For Nature listens in the rose
And hearkens in the berry's bell
To help her friends, to plague her foes,
And like wise God she judges well.
Yet doth much her love excel
To the souls that never fell,
To swains that live in happiness,
And do well because they please,
Who walk in ways that are unfamed,
And feats achieve before they're named.

R. W. Emerson

3

Lo! here the gentle lark, weary of rest,
From his moist cabinet mounts up on high,
And wakes the morning, from whose silver breast
The sun ariseth in his majesty;
    Who doth the world so gloriously behold,
    That cedar-tops and hills seem burnish'd gold.

Shakespeare

4

The lark, that shuns on lofty boughs to build
Her humble nest, lies silent in the field;
But if (the promise of a cloudless day)
Aurora smiling bids her rise and play,

Then straight she shows 'twas not for want of voice,
Or power to climb, she made so low a choice;
Singing she mounts; her airy wings are stretched
Towards heaven, as if from heaven her notes she fetched.

Edmund Waller

5

Bird of the wilderness,
Blithesome and cumberless,
Sweet be thy matin o'er moorland and lea!
Emblem of happiness,
Blest is thy dwelling-place—
Oh to abide in the desert with thee!

Wild is thy lay and loud,
Far in the downy cloud,
Love gives it energy, love gave it birth.
Where, on thy dewy wing,
Where art thou journeying?
Thy lay is in heaven, thy love is on earth.

O'er fell and fountain sheen,
O'er moor and mountain green,
O'er the red streamer that heralds the day,
Over the cloudlet dim,
Over the rainbow's rim,
Musical cherub, soar, singing, away!

Then, when the gloaming comes,
Low in the heather blooms
Sweet will thy welcome and bed of love be:
Emblem of happiness,
Blest is thy dwelling-place—
Oh to abide in the desert with thee!

James Hogg

6

How sweet is the Shepherd's sweet lot!
From the morn to the evening he strays;
He shall follow his sheep all the day,
And his tongue shall be fillèd with praise.

For he hears the lambs' innocent call,
And he hears the ewes' tender reply;
He is watchful while they are in peace,
For they know when their Shepherd is nigh.

William Blake

7

Shepherds, rise and shake off Sleep.
See the blushing Morn doth peep
Through the Window, while the Sun
To the Mountain Tops is run,
Gilding all the Vales below
With his rising Flames, which grow
Greater by his climbing still.
Up ye lazy Grooms, and fill

Bag and Bottle for the Field;
Clasp your Cloaks fast, lest they yield
To the bitter North-east Wind.
Call the Maidens up, and find
Who lay longest, that she may
Go without a Friend all Day:
Then reward your Dogs, and pray
Pan to keep you from Decay:
So unfold and then away.

John Fletcher

8

Shepherds all, and Maidens fair,
Fold your Flocks up, for the Air
'Gins to thicken, and the Sun
Already his great course hath run.
See the Dew-drops how they kiss
Ev'ry little Flower that is:
Hanging on their Velvet Heads,
Like a Rope of Cristal Beads.
See the heavy Clouds low falling,
And bright *Hesperus* down calling
The dead Night from under Ground,
At whose rising, Mists unsound,
Damps and Vapours fly apace,
Hov'ring o'er the wanton Face
Of these Pastures, where they come,
Striking dead both Bud and Bloom;

Therefore, from such Danger, lock
Ev'ry one of his loved Flock;
And let your Dogs lie loose without,
Lest the Wolf come as a scout
From the Mountain, and, e'er day,
Bear a Lamb or Kid away;
Or the crafty, thievish Fox,
Break upon your simple Flocks:
To secure your selves from these,
Be not too secure in ease;
Let one Eye his watches keep,
While the t'other Eye doth sleep;
So you shall good Shepherds prove,
And for ever hold the love
Of our great God. Sweetest Slumbers
And soft Silence fall in numbers
On your Eye-lids: So, Farewel;
Thus I end my Ev'nings knell.

John Fletcher

9

Fresh Spring the herald of loves mighty king,
    In whose cote armour richly are displayd
    All sorts of flowers the which on earth do spring
    In goodly colours gloriously arrayd,
Goe to my love, where she is carelesse layd,
    Yet in her winters bowre not wel awake:
    Tell her the joyous time wil not be staid
    Unlesse she doe him by the forelock take.

Bid her therefore her selfe soone ready make,
    To wayt on love amongst his lovely crew:
Where every one, that misseth then her make,
    Shall be by him amearst with penance dew.
Make hast therefore sweet love, whilest it is prime,
    For none can call againe the passed time.

Spenser

10

Tell me not, Sweet, I am unkind
    That from the nunnery
Of thy chaste breast and quiet mind,
    To war and arms I fly.

True, a new mistress now I chase,
    The first foe in the field;
And with a stronger faith embrace
    A sword, a horse, a shield.

Yet this inconstancy is such
    As you too shall adore;
I could not love thee, Dear, so much,
    Loved I not Honour more.

Richard Lovelace

11

Go fetch to me a pint o' wine,
    An' fill it in a silver tassie;
That I may drink, before I go,
    A service to my bonnie lassie.

March

The boat rocks at the pier o' Leith,
    Fu' loud the wind blaws frae the ferry,
The ship rides by the Berwick-law,
    And I maun leave my bonnie Mary.
The trumpets sound, the banners fly,
    The glittering spears are rankèd ready;
The shouts o' war are heard afar,
    The battle closes thick and bloody;
But it's no the roar o' sea or shore
    Wad mak me langer wish to tarry,
Nor shout o' war that's heard afar,
    It's leaving thee, my bonnie Mary.

Burns

12

Green gardens in Laventie!
    Soldiers only know the street
Where the mud is churned and splashed about
    By battle-wending feet;
And yet beside one stricken house
    There is a glimpse of grass—
Look for it when you pass.

Beyond the Church whose pitted spire
Seems balanced on a strand
Of swaying stone and tottering brick
Two roofless ruins stand;
And here, among the wreckage
    Where the back-wall should have been
We found a garden green.

The grass was never trodden on,
The little path of gravel
Was overgrown with celandine;
No other folk did travel
Along its weedy surface but the nimble-footed
    mouse
Running from house to house.

So all among the tender blades
Of soft and vivid grass
We lay, nor heard the limber wheels
That pass and ever pass
In noisy continuity until their stony rattle
    Seems in itself a battle.

At length we rose up from this ease
Of tranquil happy mind,
And searched the garden's little length
    Some new pleasaunce to find;
And there some yellow daffodils, and jasmine
    hanging high
    Did rest the tired eye.

The fairest and most fragrant
Of the many sweets we found
Was a little bush of Daphne flower
    Upon a mossy mound,
And so thick were the blossoms set and so
    divine the scent
That we were well content.

March

Hungry for Spring I bent my head,
The perfume fanned my face,
    And all my soul was dancing
In that little lovely place,
Dancing with a measured step from wrecked
        and shattered towns
    Away.....upon the Downs.

I saw green banks of daffodil,
Slim poplars in the breeze,
Great tan-brown hares in gusty March
A-courting on the leas.
And meadows, with their glittering streams—
        and silver-scurrying dace—
    Home, what a perfect place.

E. Wyndham Tennant

13

Before the winter's haunted nights are o'er,
    I thankfully rejoice, that stars look down
Above the darkened streets, and I adore
    The Heavens in London Town.

The Heavens, beneath which Alfred stood,
        when he
    Built ramparts by the tide against his foes,
The skies men loved, when in eternity
    The dreamlike Abbey rose.

The Heavens, whose glory has not known increase
    Since Ralegh swaggered home by lantern-light,
And Shakespeare looking upwards, knew the peace,
    The cool deep peace of night.

Under those Heavens brave Wesley rose betimes
    To preach ere daybreak to the tender soul;
And in the heart of Keats the starry rhymes
    Rolled, and for ever roll.

I too have walked with them the heavenly ways,—
    Tracing the sweet embroideries of the sky,
And I shall not forget, when arcs shall blaze,
    And all the lights are high.

(1915)   *Edward Shillito*

14

I heard a thousand blended notes,
While in a grove I sat reclined,
In that sweet mood when pleasant thoughts
Bring sad thoughts to the mind.

To her fair works did Nature link
The human soul that through me ran;
And much it grieved my heart to think
What man has made of man.

Through primrose tufts, in that green bower,
The periwinkle trailed its wreaths;
And 'tis my faith that every flower
Enjoys the air it breathes.

The birds around me hopped and played,
Their thoughts I cannot measure:—
But the least motion which they made,
It seem'd a thrill of pleasure.

The budding twigs spread out their fan,
To catch the breezy air;
And I must think, do all I can,
That there was pleasure there.

If this belief from heaven be sent,
If such be Nature's holy plan,
Have I not reason to lament
What man has made of man?

Wordsworth

15

The hazel-blooms, in threads of crimson hue,
Peep through the swelling buds, foretelling Spring,
Ere yet a white-thorn leaf appears in view,
Or March finds throstles pleased enough to sing.
To the old touchwood tree woodpeckers cling
A moment, and their harsh-toned notes renew;
In happier mood, the stockdove claps his wing;
The squirrel sputters up the powdered oak,
With tail cocked o'er his head, and ears erect,
Startled to hear the woodman's understroke;

And with the courage which his fears collect,
He hisses fierce half malice and half glee,
Leaping from branch to branch about the tree,
In winter's foliage, moss and lichens, deckt.

John Clare

16

Again the violet of our early days
Drinks beauteous azure from the golden sun,
And kindles into fragrance at his blaze;
The streams, rejoiced that winter's work is done,
Talk of to-morrow's cowslips, as they run.
Wild apple! thou art bursting into bloom;
Thy leaves are coming, snowy-blossomed thorn!
Wake, buried lily! spirit, quit thy tomb;
And thou, shade-loving hyacinth, be born.
Then haste, sweet rose! sweet woodbine, hymn
    the morn,
Whose dew-drops shall illume with pearly light
Each grassy blade that thick embattled stands
From sea to sea, while daisies infinite
Uplift in praise their little glowing hands
O'er every hill that under heaven expands.

Ebenezer Elliot

17

Welcome Maids of Honour
You do bring
In the Spring
And wait upon her.

March

She has Virgins many,
   Fresh and faire;
   Yet you are
More sweet then any.

Y'are the Maiden Posies,
   And so grac't,
   To be plac't,
'Fore Damask Roses.

Yet though thus respected,
   By and by
   Ye doe lie,
Poore Girles, neglected.

                      Robert Herrick

18

You meaner Beauties of the Night,
That poorly satisfie our Eyes,
More by your number, than your light,
You Common people of the Skies;
   What are you when the Moon shall rise?

You curious Chanters of the Wood,
That warble forth Dame Nature's lays,
Thinking your Passions understood
By your weak accents; what's your praise,
   When Philomel her voice shall raise?

You Violets that first appear,
By your pure purple mantles known,
Like the proud Virgins of the year,
As if the Spring were all your own;
  What are you when the Rose is blown?

So, when my Mistriss shall be seen
In Form and Beauty of her mind,
By Vertue first, then Choice, a Queen,
Tell me, if she were not design'd
  Th' Eclipse and Glory of her kind?

Sir Henry Wotton

19

She dwelt among the untrodden ways
  Beside the springs of Dove,
A Maid whom there were none to praise
  And very few to love:

A violet by a mossy stone
  Half hidden from the eye!
—Fair as a star, when only one
  Is shining in the sky.

She lived unknown, and few could know
  When Lucy ceased to be;
But she is in her grave, and, oh,
  The difference to me!

Wordsworth

20

I travelled among unknown men,
  In lands beyond the sea;
Nor, England! did I know till then
  What love I bore to thee.

'Tis past, that melancholy dream!
  Nor will I quit thy shore
A second time; for still I seem
  To love thee more and more.

Among thy mountains did I feel
  The joy of my desire;
And she I cherished turned her wheel
  Beside an English fire.

Thy mornings showed, thy nights concealed,
  The bowers where Lucy played;
And thine too is the last green field
  That Lucy's eyes surveyed.

Wordsworth

21

Now the moisty wood discloses
Wrinkled leaves of primèroses,
While the birds, they flute and sing:—
Build your nests, for here is Spring.

March

All about the open hills
Daisies shew their peasant frills,
Washed and white and newly spun
For a festival of sun.

Like a blossom from the sky,
Drops a yellow butterfly,
Dancing down the hedges grey,
Snow-bestrewn till yesterday.

Squirrels skipping up the trees,
Smell how Spring is in the breeze,
While the birds, they flute and sing:—
Build your nests, for here is Spring.

Frances Cornford

22

Aske me why I send you here
This sweet *Infanta* of the yeere?
Aske me why I send to you
This Primrose, thus bepearl'd with dew?
I will whisper to your eares,
The sweets of Love are mixt with tears.

Aske me why this flower do's show
So yellow-green, and sickly too?
Aske me why the stalk is weak
And bending, (yet it doth not break?)
I will answer, these discover
What fainting hopes are in a Lover.

Robert Herrick

23

Ye valleys low, where the mild whispers use
Of shades, and wanton winds, and gushing brooks,
On whose fresh lap the swart star sparely looks,
Throw hither all your quaint enamelled eyes,
That on the green turf suck the honied showers,
And purple all the ground with vernal flowers.
Bring the rathe primrose that forsaken dies,
The tufted crow-toe, and pale jessamine,
The white pink, and the pansy freaked with jet,
The glowing violet,
The musk-rose, and the well-attired woodbine,
With cowslips wan that hang the pensive head,
And every flower that sad embroidery wears:
Bid amaranthus all his beauty shed,
And daffadillies fill their cups with tears,
To strew the laureat hearse where Lycid lies.

Milton

24

I wandered lonely as a cloud
That floats on high o'er vales and hills,
When all at once I saw a crowd,
A host of golden daffodils;
Beside the lake, beneath the trees,
Fluttering and dancing in the breeze.

Continuous as the stars that shine
And twinkle on the milky way,
They stretched in never-ending line
Along the margin of a bay:
Ten thousand saw I at a glance,
Tossing their heads in sprightly dance.

The waves beside them danced; but they
Out-did the sparkling waves in glee:
A poet could not but be gay,
In such a jocund company:
I gazed—and gazed—but little thought
What wealth the show to me had brought:

For oft, when on my couch I lie
In vacant or in pensive mood,
They flash upon that inward eye
Which is the bliss of solitude;
And then my heart with pleasure fills,
And dances with the daffodils.

Wordsworth

25

A thing of beauty is a joy for ever:
Its loveliness increases; it will never
Pass into nothingness; but still will keep
A bower quiet for us, and a sleep
Full of sweet dreams, and health, and quiet
  breathing.
Therefore, on every morrow, are we wreathing

A flowery band to bind us to the earth,
Spite of despondence, of the inhuman dearth
Of noble natures, of the gloomy days,
Of all the unhealthy and o'er-darkened ways
Made for our searching: yes, in spite of all,
Some shape of beauty moves away the pall
From our dark spirits. Such the sun, the moon,
Trees old, and young, sprouting a shady boon
For simple sheep; and such are daffodils
With the green world they live in; and clear rills
That for themselves a cooling covert make
'Gainst the hot season; the mid forest brake,
Rich with a sprinkling of fair musk-rose blooms:
And such too is the grandeur of the dooms
We have imagined for the mighty dead;
All lovely tales that we have heard or read:
An endless fountain of immortal drink,
Pouring unto us from the heaven's brink.

Keats

26

Dip down upon the northern shore,
  O sweet new-year delaying long;
  Thou doest expectant nature wrong;
Delaying long, delay no more.

What stays thee from the clouded noons,
  Thy sweetness from its proper place?
  Can trouble live with April days,
Or sadness in the summer moons?

Bring orchis, bring the foxglove spire,
    The little speedwell's darling blue,
    Deep tulips dash'd with fiery dew,
Laburnums, dropping-wells of fire.

O thou, new-year, delaying long,
    Delayest the sorrow in my blood,
    That longs to burst a frozen bud
And flood a fresher throat with song.

Tennyson

27

To fair Fidele's grassy tomb
    Soft maids and village hinds shall bring
Each opening sweet, of earliest bloom,
    And rifle all the breathing Spring.

No wailing ghost shall dare appear
    To vex with shrieks this quiet grove,
But shepherd lads assemble here,
    And melting virgins own their love.

No wither'd witch shall here be seen,
    No goblins lead their nightly crew;
The female fays shall haunt the green,
    And dress thy grave with pearly dew.

The red-breast oft at evening hours
    Shall kindly lend his little aid,
With hoary moss, and gather'd flowers,
    To deck the ground where thou art laid.

March

When howling winds, and beating rain,
  In tempests shake the sylvan cell;
Or 'midst the chace, on every plain,
  The tender thought on thee shall dwell.

Each lovely scene shall thee restore,
  For thee the tear be duly shed;
Belov'd, till life can charm no more;
  And mourn'd, till Pity's self be dead.

William Collins

28

Oh! snatch'd away in beauty's bloom,
On thee shall press no ponderous tomb;
  But on thy turf shall roses rear
  Their leaves, the earliest of the year;
And the wild cypress wave in tender gloom:

And oft by yon blue gushing stream
  Shall Sorrow lean her drooping head;
And feed deep thought with many a dream,
  And lingering pause and lightly tread;
Fond wretch! as if her step disturb'd the dead!

Away! we know that tears are vain,
  That death nor heeds nor hears distress:
Will this unteach us to complain?
  Or make one mourner weep the less?
And thou—who tell'st me to forget,
Thy looks are wan, thine eyes are wet.

Byron

29

Ov all the birds upon the wing
Between the zunny show'rs o' spring,—
Vor all the lark, a-swingen high,
Mid zing sweet ditties to the sky,
An' sparrows, clust'rèn roun' the bough,
Mid chatter to the men at plough,—
The blackbird, whisslèn in among
The boughs, do zing the gaÿest zong.

Vor we do hear the blackbird zing
His sweetest ditties in the spring,
When nippèn win's noo mwore do blow
Vrom northern skies, wi' sleet or snow,
But drëve light doust along between
The leäne-zide hedges, thick an' green;
An' zoo the blackbird in among
The boughs do zing the gaÿest zong.

'Tis blithe, wi' newly-wakèn eyes,
To zee the mornèn's ruddy skies;
Or, out a-haulèn frith or lops
Vrom new-plësh'd hedge or new-vell'd copse,
To have woone's nammet down below
A tree where primrwosen do grow.
But there's noo time, the whole däy long,
Lik' evenèn wi' the blackbird's zong.

William Barnes

30

That same season upon a soft morning,
  Right blithe that bitter blastis were ago,
Unto the wood to see the flowers spring
  And hear the mavis sing and birdis mo,
  I passèd forth, syne lookèd to and fro,
To see the soil that was right seasonable,
Sappy, and to receive all seedis able.

Moving this gait, great mirth I took in mind
  Of labourers to see the business,
Some making dyke, and some the plough gan wind,
  Some sowing seedis fast from place to place,
  The harrowis hopping in the sowers' trace.
It was great joy to him that lovèd corn
To see them labour both at even and morn.

And as I bode under a bank full bene,[1]
  In heart greatly rejoicèd of that sight,
Unto a hedge under a hawthorn green,
  Of small birdis there came a ferly[2] flight,
  And down belyve[3] gan on the leavis light,
On every side about me where I stood,
Right marvellous, a mickle multitude.

Robert Henryson

[1] Pleasant. [2] Wondrous. [3] Quickly.

31

Within a thick and spreading hawthorn bush,
That overhung a molehill large and round,
I heard from morn to morn a merry thrush
Sing hymns of rapture, while I drank the sound
With joy—and oft, an unintruding guest,
I watched her secret toils from day to day;
How true she warped the moss to form her nest,
And modelled it within with wood and clay.
And by and by, like heath-bells gilt with dew,
There lay her shining eggs as bright as flowers,
Ink-spotted over, shells of green and blue:
And there I witnessed in the summer hours
A brood of nature's minstrels chirp and fly,
Glad as the sunshine and the laughing sky.

John Clare

APRIL

NEXT came fresh *Aprill* full of lustyhed,
  And wanton as a kid whose horne new buds:
  Upon a Bull he rode, the same which led
  Europa floting through th' *Argolick* fluds:
  His hornes were gilden all with golden studs
  And garnished with garlands goodly dight
  Of all the fairest flowres and freshest buds
  Which th' earth brings forth, and wet he seem'd
     in sight
With waves, through which he waded for his loves
    delight.

Spenser

April

I

Oh, to be in England
Now that April's there,
And whoever wakes in England
Sees, some morning, unaware,
That the lowest boughs and the brush-wood sheaf
Round the elm-tree bole are in tiny leaf,
While the chaffinch sings on the orchard bough,
In England—now!

And after April, when May follows,
And the whitethroat builds, and all the swallows!
Hark, where my blossomed pear-tree in the hedge
Leans to the field and scatters on the clover
Blossoms and dewdrops—at the bent spray's edge—
That's the wise thrush; he sings each song twice over,
Lest you should think he never could recapture
The first fine careless rapture!
And though the fields look rough with hoary dew,
All will be gay when noontide wakes anew
The buttercups, the little children's dower
—Far brighter than this gaudy melon-flower!

Robert Browning

2

Green fields of England! wheresoe'er
Across this watery waste we fare,
Your image at our hearts we bear,
Green fields of England, everywhere.

Sweet eyes in England, I must flee
Past where the wave's last confines be,
Ere your loved smile I cease to see,
Sweet eyes in England, dear to me.

Dear home in England, safe and fast
If but in thee my lot lie cast,
The past shall seem a nothing past
To thee dear home, if won at last;
Dear home in England, won at last.

A. H. Clough

3

Now the golden Morn aloft
   Waves her dew-bespangled wing,
With vermeil cheek and whisper soft
   She woos the tardy Spring:
Till April starts, and calls around
The sleeping fragrance from the ground;
And lightly o'er the living scene
Scatters his freshest, tenderest green.

New-born flocks, in rustic dance
  Frisking ply their feeble feet.
Forgetful of their wintry trance
  The Birds his presence greet.
But chief, the Sky-lark warbles high
His trembling thrilling ecstasy
And, less'ning from the dazzled sight,
Melts into air and liquid light.

Yesterday the sullen year
  Saw the snowy whirlwind fly;
Mute was the musick of the air,
  The Herd stood drooping by:
Their raptures now that wildly flow,
No yesterday, nor morrow know;
'Tis Man alone that Joy descries
With forward and reverted eyes.

Smiles on past misfortune's brow
  Soft Reflection's hand can trace;
And o'er the cheek of Sorrow throw
  A melancholy grace;
While Hope prolongs our happier hour,
Or deepest shades, that dimly lowr
And blacken round our weary way,
Gilds with a gleam of distant day.

Still, where rosy Pleasure leads,
  See a kindred grief pursue;
Behind the steps that Misery treads,
  Approaching Comfort view:

The hues of Bliss more brightly glow,
Chastised by sabler tints of woe;
And blended form, with artful strife,
The strength and harmony of Life.

See the Wretch, that long has tost
    On the thorny bed of Pain,
At length repair his vigour lost
    And breathe, and walk again:
The meanest flow'ret of the vale,
The simplest note that swells the gale,
The common Sun, the air, and skies,
To him are opening Paradise.

Thomas Gray

4

Oliver Goldsmith died April 4, 1774.

Adieu, sweet bard! to each fine feeling true,
Thy virtues many, and thy foibles few;
Those form'd to charm e'en vicious minds,—and
    these
With harmless mirth the social soul to please.
Another's woe thy heart could always melt;
None gave more free,—for none more deeply felt.
Sweet bard, adieu! thy own harmonious lays
Have sculptur'd out thy monument of praise:
Yes,—these survive to time's remotest day,
While drops the bust, and boastful tombs decay;

April

Reader, if number'd in the Muse's train,
Go, tune the lyre, and imitate his strain;
But, if no poet thou, reverse the plan,
Depart in peace, and imitate the man.

W. Woty

5

Now fades the last long streak of snow,
  Now burgeons every maze of quick
  About the flowering squares, and thick
By ashen roots the violets blow.

Now rings the woodland loud and long,
  The distance takes a lovelier hue,
  And drown'd in yonder living blue
The lark becomes a sightless song.

Now dance the lights on lawn and lea,
  The flocks are whiter down the vale,
  And milkier every milky sail
On winding stream or distant sea;

Where now the seamew pipes, or dives
  In yonder greening gleam, and fly
  The happy birds, that change their sky
To build and brood; that live their lives

From land to land; and in my breast
  Spring wakens too; and my regret
  Becomes an April violet,
And buds and blossoms like the rest.

Tennyson

6

What sweet relief the showers to thirsty plants we see,
What dear delight the blooms to bees, my true love is to
    me!
As fresh and lusty Ver foul Winter doth exceed—
As morning bright, with scarlet sky, doth pass the
    evening's weed—
As mellow pears above the crabs esteemèd be—
So doth my love surmount them all, whom yet I hap to
    see!
The oak shall olives bear, the lamb the lion fray,
The owl shall match the nightingale in tuning of her lay,
Or I my love let slip out of mine entire heart,
So deep reposèd in my breast is she for her desart!
For many blessèd gifts, O happy, happy land!
Where Mars and Pallas strive to make their glory most
    to stand
Yet, land, more is thy bliss that, in this cruel age,
A Venus' imp thou hast brought forth, so steadfast and
    so sage.
Among the Muses nine a tenth if Jove would make,
And to the Graces three a fourth, her would Apollo
    take.
Let some for honour hunt, and hoard the massy gold:
With her so I may live and die, my weal cannot be told.

                  Nicholas Grimald

7

The sun is fair when he with crimson crown,
And flaming rubies, leaves his eastern bed;
Fair is Thaumantias in her crystal gown,
When clouds engemm'd shew azure, green, and red.
To western worlds when wearied day goes down,
And from heaven's windows each star shews her head,
Earth's silent daughter, Night, is fair though brown;
Fair is the moon, though in love's livery clad.
The spring is fair when it doth paint April,
Fair are the meads, the woods, the floods are fair;
Fair looketh Ceres with her yellow hair,
And apple's queen when rose-cheek'd she doth smile.
 That heaven, and earth, and seas are fair, is true,
 Yet true, that all not please so much as you.

William Drummond

8

From you have I been absent in the spring,
When proud-pied April, dress'd in all his trim,
Hath put a spirit of youth in every thing,
That heavy Saturn laugh'd and leap'd with him.
Yet not the lays of birds, nor the sweet smell
Of different flowers in odour and in hue,
Could make me any summer's story tell,
Or from their proud lap pluck them where they grew:

Nor did I wonder at the lily's white,
Nor praise the deep vermilion in the rose;
They were but sweet, but figures of delight,
Drawn after you, you pattern of all those.
　Yet seem'd it winter still, and, you away,
　As with your shadow I with these did play.

Shakespeare

9

Though you be absent here, I needs must say,
The *Trees* as beauteous are, and *Flowers* as gay,
　As ever they were wont to be;
　Nay the *Birds* rural Musick too
　Is as melodious and free,
　As if they sung to pleasure you:
I saw a *Rose-Bud* ope this Morn; I'll swear
The blushing *Morning* open'd not more fair.

How could it be so fair, and you away?
How could the *Trees* be beauteous, *Flowers* so gay?
　Could they remember but last Year,
　How *you* did *Them, They you* delight,
　The sprouting Leaves which saw you here
　And call'd their *Fellows* to the Sight
Would, looking round for the same Sight in vain,
Creep back into their silent *Barks* again.

Abraham Cowley

10

Algernon Charles Swinburne died April 10, 1909.

Time takes them home that we loved, fair names and
    famous,
  To the soft long sleep, to the broad sweet bosom of
    death;
But the flower of their souls he shall take not away to
    shame us,
  Nor the lips lack song for ever that now lack breath.
For with us shall the music and perfume that die not dwell,
Though the dead to our dead bid welcome, and we fare-
    well.   *A. C. Swinburne*

11

'Twas on a Holy Thursday, their innocent faces clean,
The children walking two and two, in red and blue and
    green,
Grey-headed beadles walk'd before, with wands as white
    as snow,
Till into the high dome of Paul's they like Thames' waters
    flow.

O what a multitude they seem'd, these flowers of London
    town!
Seated in companies they sit with radiance all their own.
The hum of multitudes was there, but multitudes of lambs,
Thousands of little boys and girls raising their innocent
    hands.

Now like a mighty wind they raise to Heaven the voice of
    song,
Or like harmonious thunderings the seats of Heaven among.
Beneath them sit the agèd men, wise guardians of the poor;
Then cherish pity, lest you drive an angel from your door.

William Blake

12

My Soul, there is a Countrie
    Afar beyond the stars,
Where stands a wingèd Centrie
    All skilfull in the wars,
There above noise, and danger
    Sweet peace sits crown'd with smiles,
And one born in a Manger
    Commands the Beauteous files;
He is thy gracious friend,
    And (O my Soul awake!)
Did in pure love descend
    To die here for thy sake;
If thou canst get but thither,
    There growes the flowre of peace,
The Rose that cannot wither,
    Thy fortresse, and thy ease;
Leave then thy foolish ranges;
    For none can thee secure,
But one, who never changes,
    Thy God, thy life, thy cure.

Henry Vaughan

13

Sweet bird, that sing'st away the early hours
Of winter past, or coming, void of care,
Well pleased with delights which present are,
Fair seasons, budding sprays, sweet-smelling flow'rs:
To rocks, to springs, to rills, from leavy bow'rs
Thou thy Creator's goodness dost declare,
And what dear gifts on thee he did not spare,
A stain to human sense in sin that low'rs.
What soul can be so sick, which by thy songs
(Attir'd in sweetness) sweetly is not driven
Quite to forget earth's turmoils, spites, and wrongs,
And lift a reverend eye and thought to heaven?
  Sweet, artless songster, thou my mind dost raise
  To airs of spheres, yes, and to angels' lays.

William Drummond

14

I got me flowers to straw thy way,
I got me boughs off many a tree;
But Thou wast up by break of day,
And brought'st Thy sweets along with Thee.

The sunne arising in the East,
Though he give light, and th' East perfume,
If they should offer to contest
With Thy arising, they presume.

Can there be any day but this,
Though many sunnes to shine endeavour?
We count three hundred, but we misse:
There is but one, and that one ever.

George Herbert

15

Matthew Arnold died April 15, 1888.

Yes, thou art gone! and round me too the night
In ever-nearing circle weaves her shade.
I see her veil draw soft across the day,
I feel her slowly chilling breath invade
The cheek grown thin, the brown hair sprent with grey;
I feel her finger light
Laid pausefully upon life's headlong train;
The foot less prompt to meet the morning dew,
The heart less bounding at emotion new,
And hope, once crush'd, less quick to spring again.

And long the way appears, which seem'd so short
To the unpractis'd eye of sanguine youth;
And high the mountain-tops, in cloudy air,
The mountain-tops where is the throne of Truth,
Tops in life's morning-sun so bright and bare!
Unbreachable the fort
Of the long-batter'd world uplifts its wall.
And strange and vain the earthly turmoil grows,
And near and real the charm of thy repose,
And night as welcome as a friend would fall.

Matthew Arnold

16

Whan that Aprille with his shoures sote
The droghte of Marche hath perced to the rote,
And bathed every veyne in swich licour,
Of which vertu engendred is the flour;
Whan Zephirus eek with his swete breeth
Inspired hath in every holt and heeth
The tendre croppes, and the yonge sonne
Hath in the Ram his halfe cours y-ronne,
And smale fowles maken melodye,
That slepen al the night with open yë,
(So priketh hem nature in hir corages):
Than longen folk to goon on pilgrimages.

Chaucer

17

When Summer took in hand the winter to assail,
With force of might, and Virtue great, his stormy blasts
    to quail:
And when he clothèd fair the earth about with green,
And every tree new garmented, that pleasure was to
    seene:
Mine heart gan new revive, and changèd blood did stir,
Me to withdraw my winter woes, that kept within
    my dore.
'Abroad,' quoth my desire, 'assay to set thy foot
Where thou shalt find the savour sweet; for sprung is
    every root.

And to thy health, if thou wert sick in any case,
Nothing more good than in the spring the air to feel a
space.
There shalt thou hear and see all kinds of birds ywrought,
Well tune their voice with warble small, as nature hath
them taught.'
Thus prickèd me my lust the sluggish house to leave,
And for my health I thought it best such counsel to
receive.
So on a morrow forth, unwist of any wight,
I went, to prove how well it would my heavy burden
light.
And when I felt the air so pleasant round about,
Lord! to myself how glad I was that I had gotten out.
There might I see how Ver had every blossom hent,
And eke the new betrothed birds, y-coupled how they
went;
And in their songs, methought, they thankèd Nature much
That by her licence all that year to love, their hap was
such,
Right as they could devise to choose them feres[1] through-
out:
With much rejoicing to their Lord, thus flew they all
about.

Earl of Surrey

[1] Mates.

18

April, April, child of Mirth
  And Sorrow, sweetest face on earth,
  Oh! but to name thee fills mine ears
  With songs, mine eyes with pleasant tears:
  For so thou wert when I was young,
  And call'd thee with a lisping tongue,
  So wilt thou be when I am old,
  And Loves and Fears alike are cold.

Though others change, thou wilt not change;
  But alway something swift and strange,
  Like shadows follow'd by the sun,
  From thee across my heart shall run;
  While the tender breath from thee
  Sheds life o'er turf and forest tree,
  Pours love-notes through the valleys lone,
  And brings me back the swallow flown....

April, April, child of Mirth
  And Sorrow, sweetest face on earth,
  Oh! had I such bright notes to make
  The wildwoods listen for thy sake,
  Oh! had I spells to make my pains
  My glory, like thy sun-lit rains,
  My days a rainbow's arch, to climb
  Far off from tears, and clouds of Time!

                                    Frederick Tennyson

19

Lord Byron died at Missolonghi April 19, 1824.

Bards of Passion and of Mirth,
Ye have left your souls on earth!
Have ye souls in heaven too,
Double lived in regions new?
Yes, and those of heaven commune
With the spheres of sun and moon;
With the noise of fountains wond'rous,
And the parle of voices thund'rous;
With the whisper of heaven's trees
And one another, in soft ease
Seated on Elysian lawns
Brows'd by none but Dian's fawns;
Underneath large blue-bells tented,
Where the daisies are rose-scented,
And the rose herself has got
Perfume which on earth is not;
Where the nightingale doth sing
Not a senseless, tranced thing,
But divine melodious truth;
Philosophic numbers smooth;
Tales and golden histories
Of heaven and its mysteries.

Thus ye live on high, and then
On the earth ye live again;
And the souls ye left behind you
Teach us, here, the way to find you,

Where your other souls are joying,
Never slumber'd, never cloying.
Here, your earth-born souls still speak
To mortals of their little week;
Of their sorrows and delights;
Of their passions and their spites;
Of their glory and their shame;
What doth strengthen and what maim.
Thus ye teach us, every day,
Wisdom, though fled far away.

Bards of Passion and of Mirth,
Ye have left your souls on earth!
Ye have souls in heaven too,
Double-lived in regions new!

Keats

20

Hail, beauteous stranger of the grove!
Thou messenger of spring!
Now Heaven repairs thy rural seat,
And woods thy welcome sing.

What time the daisy decks the green,
Thy certain voice we hear;
Hast thou a star to guide thy path,
Or mark the rolling year?

April

Delightful visitant! with thee
I hail the time of flowers,
And hear the sound of music sweet
From birds among the bowers.

The schoolboy, wandering through the wood
To pull the primrose gay,
Starts, the new voice of spring to hear,
And imitates thy lay.

What time the pea puts on the bloom,
Thou fliest thy vocal vale,
An annual guest in other lands,
Another spring to hail.

Sweet bird! thy bower is ever green,
Thy sky is ever clear;
Thou hast no sorrow in thy song,
No winter in thy year:

Oh could I fly, I'd fly with thee!
We'd make, with joyful wing,
Our annual visit o'er the globe,
Companions of the spring.

John Logan

21

O blithe New-comer! I have heard,
I hear thee and rejoice.
O Cuckoo! shall I call thee Bird,
Or but a wandering Voice?

April

While I am lying on the grass
Thy twofold shout I hear;
From hill to hill it seems to pass
At once far off, and near.

Though babbling only to the Vale,
Of sunshine and of flowers,
Thou bringest unto me a tale
Of visionary hours.

Thrice welcome, darling of the Spring!
Even yet thou art to me
No bird, but an invisible thing,
A voice, a mystery;

The same whom in my schoolboy days
I listened to; that Cry
Which made me look a thousand ways
In bush, and tree, and sky.

To seek thee did I often rove
Through woods and on the green;
And thou wert still a hope, a love;
Still longed for, never seen.

And I can listen to thee yet;
Can lie upon the plain
And listen, till I do beget
That golden time again.

O blessèd Bird! the earth we pace
Again appears to be
An unsubstantial, faery place;
That is fit home for Thee!

Wordsworth

22

Hills and valleys where April rallies his radiant squadron
    of flowers and birds,
Steep strange beaches and lustrous reaches of fluctuant sea
    that the land engirds,
Fields and downs that the sunrise crowns with life diviner
    than lives in words,

Day by day of resurgent May salute the sun with sublime
    acclaim,
Change and brighten with hours that lighten and darken,
    girdled with cloud or flame;
Earth's fair face in alternate grace beams, blooms, and
    lowers, and is yet the same.

Twice each day the divine sea's play makes glad with
    glory that comes and goes
Field and street that her waves keep sweet, when past the
    bounds of their old repose,
Fast and fierce in renewed reverse, the foam-flecked
    estuary ebbs and flows.

Broad and bold through the stays of old staked fast with
    trunks of the wildwood tree,
Up from shoreward, impelled far forward, by marsh and
    meadow, by lawn and lea,
Inland still, at her own wild will, swells, rolls, and revels
    the surging sea.

Fair and dear is the land's face here, and fair man's work
    as a man's may be:
Dear and fair as the sunbright air is here the record that
    speaks him free;
Free by birth of a sacred Earth, and regent ever of all the
    Sea.

A. C. Swinburne

23

William Shakespeare $\begin{cases} \textit{born April 23, 1564.} \\ \textit{died April 23, 1616.} \end{cases}$
William Wordsworth died April 23, 1850.

What needs my Shakespeare for his honoured bones
The labour of an age in piled stones,
Or that his hallowed relics should be hid
Under a star-ypointing pyramid?
Dear son of memory, great heir of fame,
What need'st thou such weak witness of thy name?
Thou in our wonder and astonishment
Hast built thyself a live-long monument.
For whilst to th' shame of slow-endeavouring art,
Thy easy numbers flow, and that each heart

Hath from the leaves of thy unvalued book
Those Delphic lines with deep impression took;
Then thou, our fancy of itself bereaving,
Dost make us marble with too much conceiving;
And so sepulchered in such pomp dost lie,
That kings for such a tomb would wish to die.

Milton

And Wordsworth!—Ah, pale Ghosts, rejoice!
For never has such soothing voice
Been to your shadowy world convey'd,
Since erst, at morn, some wandering shade
Heard the clear song of Orpheus come
Through Hades, and the mournful gloom.
Wordsworth has gone from us—and ye,
Ah, may ye feel his voice as we.
He too upon a wintry clime
Had fallen—on this iron time
Of doubts, disputes, distractions, fears.
He found us when the age had bound
Our souls in its benumbing round;
He spoke, and loos'd our heart in tears.
He laid us as we lay at birth
On the cool flowery lap of earth;
Smiles broke from us and we had ease.
The hills were round us, and the breeze
Went o'er the sun-lit fields again:
Our foreheads felt the wind and rain.

Our youth return'd: for there was shed
On spirits that had long been dead,
Spirits dried up and closely-furl'd,
The freshness of the early world.

Ah, since dark days still bring to light
Man's prudence and man's fiery might,
Time may restore us in his course
Goethe's sage mind and Byron's force:
But where will Europe's latter hour
Again find Wordsworth's healing power?
Others will teach us how to dare,
And against fear our breast to steel:
Others will strengthen us to bear—
But who, ah who, will make us feel?
The cloud of mortal destiny,
Others will front it fearlessly—
But who, like him, will put it by?

Keep fresh the grass upon his grave,
O Rotha! with thy living wave.
Sing him thy best! for few or none
Hears thy voice right, now he is gone.

Matthew Arnold

24

Now, God be thanked Who has matched us with His hour,
 And caught our youth, and wakened us from sleeping,
With hand made sure, clear eye, and sharpened power,
 To turn, as swimmers into cleanness leaping,

Glad from a world grown old and cold and weary,
  Leave the sick hearts that honour could not move,
And half-men, and their dirty songs and dreary,
  And all the little emptiness of love!

Oh! we, who have known shame, we have found release
    there,
  Where there's no ill, no grief, but sleep has mending,
    Naught broken but this body, lost but breath;
Nothing to shake the laughing heart's long peace there
  But only agony, and that has ending;
    And the worst friend and enemy is but Death.

Rupert Brooke

25

Isles of the Ægean, Troy and waters of Hellespont,
  You we have known of old,
Since boyhood, stammering glorious Greek, was entranced
  In the tale that Homer told.
There scornful Achilles towered and flamed through the
    battle,
  Defying the gods; and there
Hector armed, and Andromache proudly held up his boy
    to him,
  Knowing not yet despair.

We beheld them as presences, moving beautiful and swift
 In the radiant morning of Time,
Far from reality, far from dulness of daily doing
 And from cities of fog and grime—
Unattainable day-dream, heroes, gods and goddesses,
 Matched in splendour of war,
Days of a vanished world, days of a grandeur perished,
 Days that should bloom no more!

But now shall our boyhood learn to tell a new tale,
 And a new song shall be sung,
And the sound of it shall praise not magnificence of old
  time,
 But the glory and the greatness of the young;
Deeds of this our own day, marvellous deeds of our own
  blood;
 Sons that their sires excel,
Lightly going into peril and taking death by the hand—
 Of these they shall sing, they shall tell.

How in ships sailing the famed Mediterranean
 From armed banks of Nile
Men from far homes in sunny Austral Dominions
 And the misty mother-isle
Met in the great cause, joined in the vast adventure,
 Saw first in April skies
Beyond storied islands Gallipoli's promontory,
 Impregnably ridged, arise.

And how from the belly of the black ship driven beneath
    Towering scarp and scaur,
Hailing hidden rages of fire in terrible gusts
    On the murdered space of shore,
Into the water they leapt, they rushed, and across the beach,
    With impetuous shout, all
Inspired beyond men, climbed and were over the crest
    As a flame leaps over a wall.

Not all the gods in heaven's miraculous panoply
    Could have hindered or stayed them, so
Irresistibly came they, scaled the unscaleable, and sprang
    To stab the astonished foe:
Marvellous doers of deeds, lifted past our imagining
    To a world where death is nought,
As spirit against spirit, as a liberated element,
    As fire in flesh they fought.

Now to the old twilight and pale legendary glories
    By our own youth outdone
Those shores recede; not there, but in memory everlasting
    The immortal heights were won—
Of them that triumphed, of them that fell, there is only
    now
    Silence, and sleep, and fame,
And in night's immensity, far on that promontory's altar,
    An invisibly burning flame.

Laurence Binyon

April

26

Come now, O Death,
While I am proud,
While joy and awe are breath,
And heart beats loud!

While all around me stand
Men that I love,
The wind blares aloud, the grand
Sun wheels above.

Naked I stand to-day
Before my doom,
Welcome what comes my way,
Whatever come.

What is there more to ask
Than that I have?—
Companions, love, a task,
And a deep grave!

Come then, Eternity,
If thou my lot;
Having been thus, I cannot be
As if I had not.

Naked I wait my doom!
Earth enough shroud!
Death, in thy narrow room
Man can lie proud!

Robert Nichols

27

There is a healing magic in the night,
The breeze blows cleaner than it did by day,
Forgot the fever of the fuller light,
And sorrow sinks insensibly away
As if some saint a cool white hand did lay
Upon the brow, and calm the restless brain.
The moon looks down with pale unpassioned ray—
Sufficient for the hour is its pain.
Be still and feel the night, which hides away earth's
    stain.

Be still and loose the sense of God in you,
Be still and send your soul into the all,
The vasty distance where the stars shine blue,
No longer ant-like on the earth to crawl.
Released from time and sense of great or small
Float on the pinions of the Night Queen's wings:
Soar till the swift inevitable fall
Will drag you back into all the world's small things;
Yet for an hour be one with all escaped things.

Colwyn Philipps

28

The gorse is yellow on the heath,
    The banks with speedwell flowers are gay,
The oaks are budding, and, beneath,
The hawthorn soon will bear the wreath,
    The silver wreath of May.

The welcome guest of settled Spring,
  The swallow, too, has come at last;
Just at sunset, when thrushes sing,
I saw her dash, with rapid wing,
  And hail'd her as she past.

Come, summer visitant, attach
  To my reed roof your nest of clay,
And let my ear your music catch,
Low twittering underneath the thatch
  At the grey dawn of day.

Charlotte Smith

29

The garden trees are busy with the shower
  That fell ere sunset; now methinks they talk,
Lowly and sweetly as befits the hour,
  One to another down the grassy walk.
Hark the laburnum from his opening flower
  This cherry-creeper greets in whisper light,
  While the grim fir, rejoicing in the night,
Hoarse mutters to the murmuring sycamore.
What shall I deem their converse? Would they hail
  The wild grey light that fronts yon massive cloud,
    Or the half bow, rising like pillared fire?
    Or are they sighing faintly for desire
  That with May dawn their leaves may be o'er-
    flowed,
And dews about their feet may never fail?

A. H. Hallam

30

Put forth thy leaf, thou lofty plane,
  East wind and frost are safely gone;
With zephyr mild and balmy rain
  The summer comes serenely on;
Earth, air, and sun and skies combine
  To promise all that's kind and fair:—
But thou, O human heart of mine,
  Be still, contain thyself, and bear.

December days were brief and chill,
  The winds of March were wild and drear,
And, nearing and receding still,
  Spring never would, we thought, be here.
The leaves that burst, the suns that shine,
  Had, not the less, their certain date:—
And thou, O human heart of mine,
  Be still, refrain thyself, and wait.

A. H. Clough

MAY

THEN came faire *May*, the fayrest mayd on ground,
  Deckt all with dainties of her seasons pryde,
  And throwing flowres out of her lap around:
  Upon two brethrens shoulders she did ride,
  The twinnes of *Leda*; which on eyther side
  Supported her like to their soveraine Queene.
  Lord! how all creatures laught, when her they spide,
  And leapt and daunc't as they had ravisht beene!
And *Cupid* selfe about her fluttred all in greene.

Spenser

May

I

GET up, get up for shame, the Blooming Morne
Upon her wings presents the god unshorne.
   See how *Aurora* throwes her faire
   Fresh-quilted colours through the aire:
   Get up, sweet-Slug-a-bed, and see
   The Dew-bespangling Herbe and Tree.
Each Flower has wept, and bow'd toward the East,
Above an houre since; yet you not drest,
   Nay! not so much as out of bed?
   When all the Birds have Mattens seyd,
   And sung their thankfull Hymnes: 'tis sin,
   Nay, profanation to keep in,
When as a thousand Virgins on this day,
Spring, sooner then the Lark, to fetch in May.

Rise; and put on your Foliage, and be seene
To come forth, like the Spring-time, fresh and greene;
   And sweet as *Flora*. Take no care
   For Jewels for your Gowne, or Haire:
   Feare not; the leaves will strew
   Gemms in abundance upon you:
Besides, the childhood of the Day has kept,
Against you come, some *Orient Pearls* unwept:
   Come, and receive them while the light
   Hangs on the Dew-locks of the night:
   And *Titan* on the Eastern hill
   Retires himselfe, or else stands still
Till you come forth. Wash, dresse, be briefe in praying:
Few Beads are best, when once we goe a Maying.

Come, my *Corinna*, come; and comming, marke
How each field turns a street; each street a Parke
   Made green, and trimm'd with trees: see how
   Devotion gives each House a Bough,
   Or Branch: Each Porch, each doore, ere this,
   An Arke, a Tabernacle is,
Made up of white-thorn neatly enterwove;
As if here were those cooler shades of love.
   Can such delights be in the street,
   And open fields, and we not see't?
   Come, we'll abroad; and let's obey
   The Proclamation made for May:
And sin no more, as we have done, by staying;
But my *Corinna*, come, let's goe a Maying.

There's not a budding Boy or Girle, this day,
But is got up, and gone to bring in May.
   A deale of Youth, ere this, is come
   Back, and with *White-thorn* laden home.
   Some have dispatcht their Cakes and Creame,
   Before that we have left to dreame:
And some have wept, and woo'd, and plighted Troth,
And chose their Priest, ere we can cast off sloth:
   Many a green-gown has been given;
   Many a kisse, both odde and even:
   Many a glance too has been sent
   From out the eye, Loves Firmament:
Many a jest told of the Keyes betraying
This night, and Locks pickt, yet w'are not a Maying.

May

Come, let us goe, while we are in our prime;
And take the harmlesse follie of the time.
  We shall grow old apace, and die
  Before we know our liberty.
  Our life is short; and our dayes run
  As fast away as do's the Sunne:
And as a vapour, or a drop of raine
Once lost, can ne'r be found againe:
  So when or you or I are made
  A fable, song, or fleeting shade;
  All love, all liking, all delight
  Lies drown'd with us in endlesse night.
Then while time serves, and we are but decaying;
Come, my *Corinna*, come, let's goe a Maying.

Robert Herrick

2

Now the bright morning-star, day's harbinger,
Comes dancing from the east, and leads with her
The flowery May, who from her green lap throws
The yellow cowslip and the pale primrose.
  Hail bounteous May, that dost inspire
  Mirth and youth and warm desire,
  Woods and groves are of thy dressing,
  Hill and dale doth boast thy blessing.
Thus we salute thee with our early song,
And welcome thee, and wish thee long.

Milton

3

Faire Daffadills, we weep to see
  You haste away so soone:
As yet the early-rising Sun
  Has not attain'd his Noone.
        Stay, stay,
    Untill the hasting day
        Has run
    But to the Even-song;
And, having pray'd together, we
    Will goe with you along.

We have short time to stay, as you,
  We have as short a Spring;
As quick a growth to meet Decay,
  As you, or any thing.
        We die,
    As your hours doe, and drie
        Away,
    Like to the Summers raine;
Or as the pearles of Mornings dew
    Ne'r to be found againe.

Robert Herrick

May

4

I made a posie while the day ran by:
Here will I smell my remnant out, and tie
    My life within this band;
But Time did beckon to the flow'rs, and they
By noon most cunningly did steal away,
    And wither'd in my hand.

My hand was next to them, and then my heart;
I took, without more thinking, in good part
    Time's gentle admonition;
Who did so sweetly Death's sad taste convey,
Making my minde to smell my fatall day,
    Yet sugring the suspicion.

Farewell, deare flow'rs; sweetly your time ye spent,
Fit while ye lived for smell or ornament,
    And after death for cures.
I follow straight without complaints or grief;
Since if my scent be good, I care not if
    It be as short as yours.
                    George Herbert

5

Brave flowers, that I could gallant it like you,
    And be as little vain.
You come abroad, and make a harmless show,
    And to your beds of Earth again.
You are not proud, you know your birth:
For your Embroider'd garments are from Earth.

May

You do obey your months and times, but I
    Would have it ever Spring:
My fate would know no Winter, never die,
    Nor think of such a thing.
Oh that I could my bed of Earth but view
And smile, and look as cheerfully as you!

Oh teach me to see Death and not to fear,
    But rather to take truce.
How often have I seen you at a Bier,
    And there look fresh and spruce;
You fragrant flowers then teach me, that my breath
Like yours may sweeten and perfume my death.

Henry King

6

It is not growing like a tree
    In bulk, doth make Man better be;
Or standing long an oak, three hundred year,
To fall a log at last, dry, bald, and sere:
      A lily of a day
      Is fairer far in May,
    Although it fall and die that night—
    It was the plant and flower of Light.
In small proportions we just beauties see;
And in short measures life may perfect be.

Ben Jonson

May

7

Larches all green and chestnuts hardly white,
Rough grass, and clumpy marigolds I see
Within the water: but how changed quite!
A world begins, where tree doth grow from tree.

What dusky Earths, what Fires at all compare
With thee, what Air, what Shadows lightly wrought,
Thou living Water! Settled softly there,
Proud with the proud reality of Thought.

Francis Békassy

8

When I did wake this morn from sleep,
　It seemed I heard birds in a dream;
Then I arose to take the air—
　The lovely air that made birds scream;
Just as a green hill launched the ship
Of gold, to take its first clear dip.

And it began its journey then,
　As I came forth to take the air;
The timid Stars had vanished quite,
　The Moon was dying with a stare;
Horses, and kine, and sheep were seen
As still as pictures, in fields green.

It seemed as though I had surprised
  And trespassed in a golden world
That should have passed while men still slept!
  The joyful birds, the ship of gold,
The horses, kine and sheep did seem
As they would vanish for a dream.

W. H. Davies

9

This day dame Nature seem'd in love;
The lusty sap began to move;
Fresh juice did stir th' embracing vines;
And birds had drawn their valentines.
The jealous trout, that low did lie,
Rose at a well-dissembled fly;
There stood my friend, with patient skill,
Attending of his trembling quill;
Already were the eaves possess'd
With the swift pilgrim's daubèd nest;
The groves already did rejoice
In Philomel's triumphing voice,
The showers were short, the weather mild,
The morning fresh, the evening smiled.
  Joan takes her neat-rubb'd pail, and now
She trips to milk the sand-red cow;
Where, for some sturdy foot-ball swain,
Joan strokes a syllabub or twain.
The fields and gardens were beset
With tulip, crocus, violet;

And now, though late, the modest rose
Did more than half a blush disclose.
 Thus all looks gay and full of cheer,
 To welcome the new-liveried year.

        Sir Henry Wotton

10

Spring, the sweet Spring, is the year's pleasant king;
Then blooms each thing, then maids dance in a ring,
Cold doth not sting, the pretty birds do sing—
 Cuckoo, jug-jug, pu-we, to-witta-woo!

The palm and may make country houses gay,
Lambs frisk and play, the shepherds pipe all day,
And we hear aye birds tune this merry lay—
 Cuckoo, jug-jug, pu-we, to-witta-woo!

The fields breathe sweet, the daisies kiss our feet,
Young lovers meet, old wives a-sunning sit,
In every street these tunes our ears do greet—
 Cuckoo, jug-jug, pu-we, to-witta-woo!
 Spring, the sweet Spring!

        Thomas Nashe

11

The lark now leaves his wat'ry nest,
 And climbing shakes his dewy wings.
He takes this window for the East,
 And to implore your light he sings—
Awake, awake! The morn will never rise
Till she can dress her beauty at your eyes.

The merchant bows unto the seaman's star,
  The ploughman from the sun his season takes;
But still the lover wonders what they are
  Who look for day before his mistress wakes.
Awake, awake! break through your veils of lawn!
Then draw your curtains, and begin the Dawn!

Sir William Davenant

12

Hark! hark! the lark at heaven's gate sings,
  And Phoebus 'gins arise,
His steeds to water at those springs
  On chalic'd flowers that lies;
And winking Mary-buds begin
  To ope their golden eyes:
With every thing that pretty is,
  My lady sweet, arise:
    Arise, arise!

Shakespeare

13

Ethereal minstrel! pilgrim of the sky!
Dost thou despise the earth where cares abound?
Or, while the wings aspire, are heart and eye
Both with thy nest upon the dewy ground?
Thy nest which thou canst drop into at will,
Those quivering wings composed, that music still!

To the last point of vision, and beyond,
Mount, daring warbler! that love-prompted strain,
('Twixt thee and thine a never-failing bond,)
Thrills not the less the bosom of the plain:
Yet mightst thou seem, proud privilege! to sing
All independent of the leafy spring.

Leave to the nightingale her shady wood;
A privacy of glorious light is thine;
Whence thou dost pour upon the world a flood
Of harmony, with instinct more divine;
Type of the wise who soar, but never roam;
True to the kindred points of Heaven and Home!

Wordsworth

14

When in disgrace with fortune and men's eyes,
I all alone beweep my outcast state,
And trouble deaf heaven with my bootless cries,
And look upon myself, and curse my fate,
Wishing me like to one more rich in hope,
Featur'd like him, like him with friends possess'd,
Desiring this man's art, and that man's scope,
With what I most enjoy contented least;
Yet in these thoughts myself almost despising,
Haply I think on thee,—and then my state,

Like to the lark at break of day arising
From sullen earth, sings hymns at heaven's gate;
 For thy sweet love remember'd such wealth brings
 That then I scorn to change my state with kings.

Shakespeare

15

The soote season, that bud and bloom forth brings,
With green hath clad the hill and eke the vale.
The nightingale with feathers new she sings;
The turtle to her make hath told her tale.
Summer is come, for every spray now springs.
The hart hath hung his old head on the pale;
The buck in brake his winter coat he flings;
The fishes flete with new repaired scale;
The adder all her slough away she slings;
The swift swallow pursueth the flies smale;
The busy bee her honey now she mings;
Winter is worn that was the flowers' bale.

And thus I see among these pleasant things
Each care decays, and yet my sorrow springs!

Earl of Surrey

16

And on the small grene twistis sate
The lytil suete nyghtingale, and song
So loud and clere, the ympnis consecrat
Of luvis use, now soft now loud among,

That all the gardynis and the wallis rong
Ryt of thaire song, and on the copill next
Of thaire suete armony, and lo the text:

  Worschippe ye that loveris bene this May,
For of your bliss the kalendis are begonne,
And sing with us, Away winter, away!
Come somer, come, the suete seson and sonne!
Awake, for schame! that have your hevynis wonne,
And amourously lift up your hedis all—
Thank lufe that list you to his merci call.

King James I of Scotland

17

As it fell upon a day
In the merry month of May,
Sitting in a pleasant shade
Which a grove of myrtles made,
Beasts did leap and birds did sing,
Trees did grow and plants did spring,
Everything did banish moan
Save the nightingale alone.
She, poor bird, as all forlorn,
Lean'd her breast against a thorn,
And there sung the dolefullest ditty
That to hear it was great pity.
Fie, fie, fie, now would she cry;
Tereu, tereu, by and by:
That to hear her so complain
Scarce I could from tears refrain;

For her griefs so lively shown
Made me think upon mine own.
—Ah, thought I, thou mournst in vain,
None takes pity on thy pain:
Senseless trees, they cannot hear thee,
Ruthless beasts, they will not cheer thee;
King Pandion, he is dead,
All thy friends are lapp'd in lead:
All thy fellow birds do sing
Careless of thy sorrowing:
Even so, poor bird, like thee
None alive will pity me.

Richard Barnefield

18

Now came still Evening on, and Twilight grey
Had in her sober livery all things clad;
Silence accompanied; for beast and bird,
They to their grassy couch, these to their nests
Were slunk, all but the wakeful nightingale;
She all night long her amorous descant sung:
Silence was pleased. Now glowed the firmament
With living sapphires; Hesperus, that led
The starry host, rode brightest, till the Moon,
Rising in clouded majesty, at length
Apparent queen, unveiled her peerless light,
And o'er the dark her silver mantle threw.

Milton

19

My heart aches, and a drowsy numbness pains
  My sense, as though of hemlock I had drunk,
Or emptied some dull opiate to the drains
  One minute past, and Lethewards had sunk:
'Tis not through envy of thy happy lot,
  But being too happy in thy happiness,—
    That thou, light-winged Dryad of the trees,
      In some melodious plot
  Of beechen green, and shadows numberless,
    Singest of summer in full-throated ease.

O for a draught of vintage! that hath been
  Cool'd a long age in the deep-delvèd earth,
Tasting of Flora and the country green,
  Dance, and Provençal song, and sunburnt mirth!
O for a beaker full of the warm South,
  Full of the true, the blushful Hippocrene,
    With beaded bubbles winking at the brim,
      And purple-stainèd mouth;
  That I might drink, and leave the world unseen,
    And with thee fade away into the forest dim:

Fade far away, dissolve, and quite forget
  What thou among the leaves hast never known,
The weariness, the fever, and the fret
  Here, where men sit and hear each other groan;
Where palsy shakes a few, sad, last grey hairs,
  Where youth grows pale, and spectre-thin, and dies;

Where but to think is to be full of sorrow
And leaden-eyed despair,
Where Beauty cannot keep her lustrous eyes,
Or new Love pine at them beyond to-morrow.

Away! away! for I will fly to thee,
Not charioted by Bacchus and his pards,
But on the viewless wings of Poesy,
Though the dull brain perplexes and retards:
Already with thee! tender is the night,
And haply the Queen-Moon is on her throne,
Cluster'd around by all her starry Fays;
But here there is no light,
Save what from heaven is with the breezes blown
Through verdurous glooms and winding mossy ways.

I cannot see what flowers are at my feet,
Nor what soft incense hangs upon the boughs,
But, in embalmed darkness, guess each sweet
Wherewith the seasonable month endows
The grass, the thicket, and the fruit-tree wild;
White hawthorn, and the pastoral eglantine;
Fast-fading violets cover'd up in leaves;
And mid-May's eldest child,
The coming musk-rose, full of dewy wine,
The murmurous haunt of flies on summer eves.

Darkling I listen; and, for many a time
I have been half in love with easeful Death,
Call'd him soft names in many a mused rhyme,
To take into the air my quiet breath;

9—2

Now more than ever seems it rich to die,
To cease upon the midnight with no pain,
While thou art pouring forth thy soul abroad
In such an ecstasy!
Still wouldst thou sing, and I have ears in vain—
To thy high requiem become a sod.

Thou wast not born for death, immortal Bird!
No hungry generations tread thee down;
The voice I hear this passing night was heard
In ancient days by emperor and clown:
Perhaps the self-same song that found a path
Through the sad heart of Ruth, when, sick for home,
She stood in tears amid the alien corn;
The same that oft-times hath
Charm'd magic casements, opening on the foam
Of perilous seas, in faery lands forlorn.

Forlorn! the very word is like a bell
To toll me back from thee to my sole self!
Adieu! the Fancy cannot cheat so well
As she is fam'd to do, deceiving elf.
Adieu! Adieu! thy plaintive anthem fades
Past the near meadows, over the still stream,
Up the hill-side; and now 'tis buried deep
In the next valley-glades:
Was it a vision, or a waking dream?
Fled is that music: Do I wake or sleep?

Keats

20

Faire pledges of a fruitfull Tree,
  Why do yee fall so fast?
  Your date is not so past
But you may stay yet here a while,
  To blush and gently smile;
      And go at last.

What, were yee borne to be
  An houre or half's delight;
  And so to bid goodnight?
'Twas pitie Nature brought yee forth
  Meerly to shew your worth,
      And lose you quite.

But you are lovely Leaves, where we
  May read how soon things have
  Their end, though ne'r so brave:
And after they have shown their pride,
  Like you a while: They glide
      Into the Grave.

                              Robert Herrick

21

A country life is sweet;
  In moderate cold and heat,
To walk in the air how pleasant and fair,
  In every field of wheat,

May

The fairest of flowers adorning the bowers,
  And every meadow's brow;
So that I say, no courtier may
Compare with they who clothe in gray,
  And follow the useful plough.

They rise with the morning lark,
  And labour till almost dark,
Then folding their sheep, they hasten to sleep;
  While every pleasant park
Next morning is ringing with birds that are singing
  On each green, tender bough.
With what content and merriment
Their days are spent, whose minds are bent
  To follow the useful plough!

Anon

22

Oh! I be shepherd o' the farm,
  Wi' tinklèn bells an' sheep-dog's bark,
An' wi' my crook a-thirt my eärm,
  Here I do rove below the lark.

An' I do bide all day among
  The bleäten sheep, an' pitch their vwold;
An' when the evenen sheädes be long,
  Do zee em all a-penn'd an' twold.

May

An' I do zee the friskèn lam's,
  Wi' swingèn tails an' woolly lags,
A-playèn roun' their veedèn dams,
  An' pullèn o' their milky bags.

An' I bezide a hawthorn tree,
  Do zit upon the zunny down,
While sheädes o' zummer clouds do vlee
  Wi' silent flight along the groun'.

An' there, among the many cries
  O' sheep an' lam's, my dog da pass
A zultry hour wi' blinken eyes,
  An' nose a-stratch'd upon the grass.

But in a twinklen, at my word,
  The shaggy rogue is up an' gone
Out roun' the sheep lik' any bird,
  To do what he's a-zent upon.

An' wi' my zong, an wi' my fife,
  An wi' my hut o' turf an' hurdles,
I wou'den channge my shepherd's life
  To be a-miade a king o' wordles.

An' I da goo to washen pool,
  A-sousen auver head an' ears
The shaggy sheep, to cleän ther wool,
  An' miake 'em ready var the shears.

An' when the shearen time da come,
  I be at barn vrom dawn till dark,
Wher zome da catch the sheep, and zome
  Da mark ther zides wi' miaster's mark.

An' when the shearen's al a-done,
  Then we da eat, an' drink, an' zing
In miaster's kitchen, till the tun
  Wi' merry sounds da shiake an' ring.

I be the shepherd o' the farm:
  An' be so proud a-roven round
Wi' my long crook a-thirt my yarm,
  As ef I were a king a-crown'd.

William Barnes

23

In the door-yard fronting an old farm-house near the
  whitewashed palings,
Stands the lilac bush, tall-growing, with heart-shaped leaves
  of rich green,
With many a pointed blossom, rising delicate, with the
  perfume strong I love,
With every leaf a miracle: and from this bush in the door-
  yard,
With delicate-coloured blossoms, and heart-shaped leaves
  of rich green,
A sprig, with its flower, I break.

Walt Whitman

24

Her court was pure; her life serene;
　　God gave her peace; her land reposed
　　A thousand claims to reverence closed
In her as Mother, Wife, and Queen;

And statesmen at her council met
　　Who knew the seasons when to take
　　Occasion by the hand, and make
The bounds of freedom wider yet

By shaping some august decree,
　　Which kept her throne unshaken still,
　　Broad-based upon her people's will,
And compass'd by the inviolate sea.

　　　　　　　　　　Tennyson

25

Shall I compare thee to a summer's day?
Thou art more lovely and more temperate:
Rough winds do shake the darling buds of May,
And summer's lease hath all too short a date:
Sometime too hot the eye of heaven shines,
And often is his gold complexion dimm'd;
And every fair from fair sometime declines,
By chance, or nature's changing course untrimm'd;

But thy eternal summer shall not fade,
Nor lose possession of that fair thou ow'st;
Nor shall death brag thou wander'st in his shade,
When in eternal lines to time thou grow'st;
   So long as men can breathe, or eyes can see,
   So long lives this, and this gives life to thee.

Shakespeare

26

My banks they are furnish'd with bees,
   Whose murmur invites one to sleep;
My grottoes are shaded with trees,
   And my hills are white over with sheep.
I seldom have met with a loss,
   Such health do my fountains bestow;
My fountains all border'd with moss,
   Where the hare-bells and violets grow.

Not a pine in the grove is there seen,
   But with tendrils of woodbine is bound:
Not a beech's more beautiful green
   But a sweet-briar entwines it around.
Not my fields, in the prime of the year,
   More charms than my cattle unfold;
Not a brook that is limpid and clear,
   But it glitters with fishes of gold.

May

One would think she might like to retire
   To the bower I have labour'd to rear;
Not a shrub that I heard her admire,
   But I hasted and planted it there.
O how sudden the jessamine strove
   With the lilac to render it gay!
Already it calls for my love
   To prune the wild branches away.

I have found out a gift for my fair;
   I have found where the wood-pigeons breed:
But let me that plunder forbear,
   She will say 'twas a barbarous deed:
For he ne'er could be true, she aver'd,
   Who could rob a poor bird of its young:
And I lov'd her the more when I heard
   Such tenderness fall from her tongue.

William Shenstone

27

The pinks along my garden walks
Have all shot forth their summer stalks,
Thronging their buds 'mong tulips hot,
   And blue forget-me-not.

Their dazzling snows forth bursting soon
Will lade the idle breath of June:
And waken through the fragrant night
   To steal the pale moonlight.

May

The nightingale at end of May
Lingers each year for their display;
Till when he sees their blossoms blown,
    He knows the spring is flown.

June's birth they greet, and when their bloom
Dislustres, withering on his tomb,
Then summer hath a shortening day;
    And steps slow to decay.

Robert Bridges

28

And Zephirus and Flora gentilly
Yaf to the floures, softe and tenderly,
Hir swote breth, and made hem for to sprede,
As god and goddesse of the floury mede;
In which me thoghte I mighte, day by day,
Dwellen alwey, the joly month of May,
Withouten sleep, withouten mete or drinke.
A-doun ful softely I gan to sinke;
And, leninge on myn elbowe and my syde,
The longe day I shoop me for to abyde
For nothing elles, and I shal nat lye,
But for to loke upon the dayesye,
That wel by reson men hit calle may
The 'dayesye' or elles the 'ye of day,'
The emperice and flour of floures alle;
I pray to god that faire mot she falle,
And alle that loven floures, for hir sake!

Chaucer

29

Shut not so soon; the dull-ey'd night
   Ha 's not as yet begunne
To make a seisure on the light,
   Or to seale up the Sun.

No Marigolds yet closed are;
   No shadowes great appeare;
Nor doth the early Shepheards Starre
   Shine like a spangle here.

Stay but till my *Julia* close
   Her life-begetting eye;
And let the whole world then dispose
   It selfe to live or dye.

                Robert Herrick

30

The noon was shady, and soft airs
   Swept Ouse's silent tide,
When, 'scap'd from literary cares,
   I wander'd on his side.

My spaniel, prettiest of his race,
   And high in pedigree,
(Two nymphs, adorn'd with ev'ry grace,
   That spaniel found for me)

May

Now wanton'd lost in flags and reeds,
   Now starting into sight,
Pursued the swallow o'er the meads
   With scarce a slower flight.

It was the time when Ouse display'd
   His lilies newly blown;
Their beauties I intent survey'd;
   And one I wish'd my own.

With cane extended far I sought
   To steer it close to land;
But still the prize, though nearly caught,
   Escap'd my eager hand.

Beau marked my unsuccessful pains
   With fixt consid'rate face,
And puzzling set his puppy brains
   To comprehend the case.

But with a chirrup clear and strong,
   Dispersing all his dream,
I thence withdrew, and follow'd long
   The windings of the stream.

My ramble finish'd, I return'd.
   Beau trotting far before
The floating wreath again discern'd,
   And plunging left the shore.

I saw him with that lily cropp'd
   Impatient swim to meet
My quick approach, and soon he dropp'd
   The treasure at my feet.

Charm'd with the sight, 'the world,' I cried,
   'Shall hear of this thy deed,
My dog shall mortify the pride
   Of man's superior breed;

'But chief, myself I will enjoin,
   Awake at duty's call,
To show a love as prompt as thine
   To Him who gives me all.'

William Cowper

31

When May is in his prime,
   Then may each heart rejoice:
When May bedecks each branch with green,
   Each bird strains forth his voice.

The lively sap creeps up
   Into the blooming thorn:
The flowers, which close in prison kept,
   Now laugh the frost to scorn.

All nature's imps triumph
   Whiles joyful May doth last;
When May is gone, of all the year
   The pleasant time is past.

May

May makes the cheerful hue,
   May breeds and brings new blood,
May marches throughout every limb,
   May makes the merry mood.

May pricketh tender hearts
   Their warbling notes to tune.
Full strange it is, yet some, we see,
   Do make their May in June.

Thus things are strangely wrought
   Whiles joyful May doth last.
Take May in time: when May is gone,
   The pleasant time is past.

All ye that live on earth,
   And have your May at will,
Rejoice in May, as I do now,
   And use your May with skill.

Use May while that you may,
   For May hath but his time;
When all the fruit is gone, it is
   Too late the tree to climb.

Your liking and your lust
   Is fresh while May doth last:
When May is gone, of all the year
   The pleasant time is past.

Richard Edwardes

JUNE

AND after her, came jolly *June*, arrayd
   All in greene leaves, as he a Player were;
   Yet in his time, he wrought as well as playd,
   That by his plough-yrons mote right well appeare;
   Upon a Crab he rode, that him did beare
   With crooked crawling steps an uncouth pase,
   And backward yode, as Bargemen wont to fare
   Bending their force contrary to their face,
Like that ungracious crew which faines demurest
     grace.

Spenser

June

I

It was the azure time of June,
When the skies are deep in the stainless noon,
And the warm and fitful breezes shake
The fresh green leaves of the hedgerow briar,
And there were odours then to make
The very breath we did respire
A liquid element, whereon
Our spirits, like delighted things
That walk the air on subtle wings,
Floated and mingled far away,
'Mid the warm winds of the sunny day.
And when the evening star came forth
Above the curve of the new bent moon,
And light and sound ebbed from the earth,
Like the tide of the full and weary sea
To the depths of its own tranquillity,
Our natures to its own repose
Did the Earth's breathless sleep attune.

Shelley

2

Sweet day, so cool, so calm, so bright,
The bridall of the earth and skie,
The dew shall weep thy fall to-night;
       For thou must die.

Sweet rose, whose hue angrie and brave
Bids the rash gazer wipe his eye,
Thy root is ever in its grave,
    And thou must die.

Sweet spring, full of sweet days and roses,
A box where sweets compacted lie,
My musick shows ye have your closes,
    And all must die.

Onely a sweet and vertuous soul,
Like season'd timber, never gives;
But though the whole world turn to coal,
    Then chiefly lives.

George Herbert

3

I gazed upon the glorious sky
 And the green mountains round;
And thought that when I came to lie
 At rest within the ground,
'Twere pleasant, that in flowery June,
When brooks send up a cheerful tune,
 And groves a joyous sound,
The sexton's hand, my grave to make,
The rich, green mountain turf should break.

June

A cell within the frozen mould,
  A coffin borne through sleet,
And icy clods above it rolled,
  While fierce the tempests beat—
Away:—I will not think of these—
Blue be the sky and soft the breeze,
  Earth green beneath the feet,
And be the damp mould gently pressed
Into my narrow place of rest.

There through the long, long summer hours,
  The golden light should lie,
And thick young herbs and groups of flowers
  Stand in their beauty by.
The oriole should build and tell
His love-tale close beside my cell;
  The idle butterfly
Should rest him there, and there be heard
The housewife bee and humming-bird.

And what if cheerful sounds at noon
  Come, from the village sent,
Or songs of maids, beneath the moon
  With fairy laughter blent?
And what if, in the evening light,
Betrothed lovers walk in sight
  Of my low monument?
I would the lovely scene around
Might know no sadder sight nor sound.

I know, I know I should not see
 The season's glorious show,
Nor would its brightness shine for me,
 Nor its wild music flow;
But if, around my place of sleep,
The friends I love should come to weep,
 They might not haste to go.
Soft airs, and song, and light, and bloom,
Should keep them lingering by my tomb.

These to their softened hearts should bear
 The thought of what has been,
And speak of one who cannot share
 The gladness of the scene;
Whose part, in all the pomp that fills
The circuit of the summer hills,
 Is—that his grave is green;
And deeply would their hearts rejoice
To hear again his living voice.

       W. C. Bryant

4

The evening comes, the field is still.
The tinkle of the thirsty rill,
Unheard all day, ascends again;
Deserted is the new-reap'd grain,
Silent the sheaves! the ringing wain,
The reaper's cry, the dog's alarms,
All housed within the sleeping farms!

June

The business of the day is done,
The last belated gleaner gone.
And from the thyme upon the height,
And from the elder-blossom white
And pale dog-roses in the hedge,
And from the mint-plant in the sedge,
In puffs of balm the night-air blows
The perfume which the day forgoes.
And on the pure horizon far,
See, pulsing with the first-born star,
The liquid sky above the hill!
The evening comes, the field is still.

Matthew Arnold

5

'I fear thee, ancient Mariner!'
'Be calm, thou Wedding-Guest!
'Twas not those souls that fled in pain,
Which to their corses came again,
But a troop of spirits blest:

For when it dawned—they dropped their arms,
And clustered round the mast;
Sweet sounds rose slowly through their mouths,
And from their bodies passed.

Around, around, flew each sweet sound,
Then darted to the Sun;
Slowly the sounds came back again,
Now mixed, now one by one.

Sometimes a-dropping from the sky
I heard the sky-lark sing;
Sometimes all little birds that are,
How they seemed to fill the sea and air
With their sweet jargoning!

And now 'twas like all instruments,
Now like a lonely flute;
And now it is an angel's song,
That makes the heavens be mute.

It ceased; yet still the sails made on
A pleasant noise till noon,
A noise like of a hidden brook
In the leafy month of June,
That to the sleeping woods all night
Singeth a quiet tune.'

S. T. Coleridge

6

Eftsoones they heard a most melodious sound,
  Of all that mote delight a daintie eare,
  Such as attonce might not on living ground,
  Save in this Paradise, be heard elswhere:
  Right hard it was, for wight, which did it heare,
  To read, what manner musicke that mote bee:
  For all that pleasing is to living eare,
  Was there consorted in one harmonee,
Birdes, voyces, instruments, windes, waters, all agree.

The joyous birdes, shrouded in chearefull shade,
　Their notes unto the voyce attempred sweet;
Th' Angelicall soft trembling voyces made
To th' instruments divine respondence meet:
The silver sounding instruments did meet
With the base murmure of the waters fall:
The waters fall with difference discreet,
　Now soft, now loud, unto the wind did call:
The gentle warbling wind low answered to all.

Spenser

7

　I loked forth, for I was waked
With smale foules a gret hepe,
That had affrayed me out of slepe
Through noyse and swetnesse of hir song;
And, as me mette, they sate among,
Upon my chambre-roof withoute,
Upon the tyles, al a-boute,
And songen, everich in his wyse,
The moste solempne servyse
By note, that ever man, I trowe,
Had herd; for som of hem song lowe,
Som hye, and al of oon acorde
To telle shortly, at oo worde,
Was never y-herd so swete a steven,
But hit had be a thing of heven.

Chaucer

8

Green little vaulter in the sunny grass,
 Catching your heart up at the feel of June,
 Sole voice that's heard amidst the lazy noon,
When even the bees lag at the summoning brass;
And you, warm little housekeeper, who class
 With those who think the candles come too soon,
 Loving the fire, and with your tricksome tune
Nick the glad silent moments as they pass;
Oh sweet and tiny cousins, that belong,
 One to the fields, the other to the hearth,
Both have your sunshine; both, though small, are strong
 At your clear hearts; and both seem given to earth
To sing in thoughtful ears this natural song—
 In doors and out, summer and winter, Mirth.

         Leigh Hunt

9

Happy *Insect*, what can be
In Happiness compar'd to thee?
Fed with Nourishment Divine,
The dewy Morning's gentle Wine!
Nature waits upon thee still,
And thy verdant Cup does fill;
'Tis fill'd where-ever thou dost tread,
Nature self's thy *Ganymede*.

Thou dost drink, and dance, and sing;
Happier than the happiest King!
All the *Fields*, which thou dost see,
All the *Plants* belong to *Thee*,
All that Summer Hours produce,
Fertile made with early Juice.
Man for thee does sow and plough;
Farmer He, and *Landlord Thou!*

Abraham Cowley

10

I've watched you now a full half-hour,
Self-poised upon that yellow flower;
And, little Butterfly! indeed
I know not if you sleep or feed.
How motionless! not frozen seas
More motionless! and then
What joy awaits you, when the breeze
Hath found you out among the trees,
And calls you forth again!

This plot of orchard-ground is ours;
My trees they are, my Sister's flowers;
Here rest your wings when they are weary;
Here lodge as in a sanctuary!
Come often to us, fear no wrong;
Sit near us on the bough!

We'll talk of sunshine and of song,
And summer days, when we were young;
Sweet childish days, that were as long
As twenty days are now.

Wordsworth

II

O BLACKBIRD! sing me something well:
  While all the neighbours shoot thee round,
  I keep smooth plats of fruitful ground,
Where thou may'st warble, eat and dwell.

The espaliers and the standards all
  Are thine; the range of lawn and park:
  The unnetted black-hearts ripen dark,
All thine, against the garden wall.

Yet, tho' I spared thee all the spring,
  Thy sole delight is, sitting still,
  With that gold dagger of thy bill
To fret the summer jenneting.

A golden bill! the silver tongue,
  Cold February loved, is dry:
  Plenty corrupts the melody
That made thee famous once, when young:

And in the sultry garden-squares,
  Now thy flute-notes are changed to coarse,
  I hear thee not at all, or hoarse
As when a hawker hawks his wares.

Take warning! he that will not sing
　　While yon sun prospers in the blue,
　　Shall sing for want, ere leaves be new,
Caught in the frozen palms of Spring.

Tennyson

12

So, some tempestuous morn in early June,
　　When the year's primal burst of bloom is o'er,
　　Before the roses and the longest day—
　　When garden-walks, and all the grassy floor,
　　　With blossoms, red and white, of fallen May,
　　　And chestnut-flowers are strewn—
So have I heard the cuckoo's parting cry,
　　From the wet field, through the vext garden-trees,
　　Come with the volleying rain and tossing breeze:
The bloom is gone, and with the bloom go I.

Too quick despairer, wherefore wilt thou go?
　　Soon will the high Midsummer pomps come on,
　　　Soon will the musk carnations break and swell,
　　Soon shall we have gold-dusted snapdragon, 　.
　　　Sweet-William with its homely cottage-smell,
　　　　And stocks in fragrant blow;
　　Roses that down the alleys shine afar,
　　　And open, jasmine-muffled lattices,
　　　And groups under the dreaming garden-trees,
　　And the full moon, and the white evening-star.

Matthew Arnold

13

When in the woods I wander all alone,
The woods that are my solace and delight,
Which I more covet than a prince's throne,
My toil by day and canopy by night;
(Light heart, light foot, light food, and slumber light,
These lights shall light me to old age's gate,
While monarchs, whom rebellious dreams affright,
Heavy with fear, death's fearful summons wait;)
Whilst here I wander, pleased to be alone,
Weighing in thought the world's no-happiness,
I cannot choose but wonder at its moan,
Since so plain joys the woody life can bless:
Then live who may where honied words prevail,
I with the deer, and with the nightingale!

Lord Thurlow

14

Come live with me and be my Love,
And we will all the pleasures prove
That hills and valleys, dale and field,
And all the craggy mountains yield;

There will we sit upon the rocks
And see the shepherds feed their flocks,
By shallow rivers, to whose falls
Melodious birds sing madrigals.

There will I make thee beds of roses
And a thousand fragrant posies,
A cap of flowers, and a kirtle
Embroider'd all with leaves of myrtle;

A gown made of the finest wool,
Which from our pretty lambs we pull,
Fair linèd slippers for the cold,
With buckles of the purest gold;

A belt of straw and ivy buds,
With coral clasps and amber studs:
And if these pleasures may thee move,
Come live with me and be my Love.

Thy silver dishes for thy meat
As precious as the gods do eat,
Shall on an ivory table be
Prepared each day for thee and me.

The shepherd swains shall dance and sing
For thy delight each May-morning:
If these delights thy mind may move,
Then live with me and be my Love.

Christopher Marlowe

15

The damask meddowes, and the crawlinge streames,
  Sweeten, and make soft thy dreams.
The purlinge springes, groves, birdes, and well-weav'd
    bowers,
  With fields enamelled with flowers,

Present thee shapes, while phantasye discloses
  Millions of lillyes mixt with roses.
Then dreame thou hear'st the lambe with many a bleat
  Woo'd to come sucke the milkey teate;
Whilst Faunus, in the vision, vowes to keepe
  From ravenouse wolfe the woolley sheepe;
With thowsand such enchantinge dreames, which meet
  To make sleepe not so sound as sweet.
Nor can these figures in thy rest endeere,
  As not to up when chanticleere
Speaks the last watch, but with the dawne dost rise
  To worke, but first to sacrifice:
Making thy peace with Heaven for some late fault,
  With holy meale, and cracklinge salt.
That done, thy painful thumbe this sentence tells us,
  God for our labour all things sells us.
Nor are thy dayle and devout affayres
  Attended with those desperate cares
Th' industriouse merchant hath, who for to finde
  Gold, runneth to the furthest Inde,
And home againe tortur'd with fear doth hye
  Untaught to suffer povertye.

                 Richard Corbet

16

  O Solitude! if I must with thee dwell,
    Let it not be among the jumbled heap
    Of murky buildings: climb with me the steep,—
  Nature's observatory—whence the dell,

Its flowery slopes, its river's crystal swell,
  May seem a span; let me thy vigils keep
    'Mongst boughs pavilion'd, where the deer's swift leap
Startles the wild bee from the foxglove bell.
  But though I'll gladly trace these scenes with thee,
  Yet the sweet converse of an innocent mind,
Whose words are images of thoughts refined,
  Is my soul's pleasure; and it sure must be
Almost the highest bliss of human-kind,
  When to thy haunts two kindred spirits flee.

Keats

17

  Be full, ye courts! be great who will;
Search for Peace with all your skill:
Open wide the lofty door,
Seek her on the marble floor:
In vain you search, she is not there;
In vain ye search the domes of Care!
Grass and flowers Quiet treads,
On the meads and mountain-heads,
Along with Pleasure close allied,
Ever by each other's side;
And often, by the murm'ring rill,
Hears the thrush, while all is still,
Within the groves of Grongar Hill.

John Dyer

18

There was a sound of revelry by night,
And Belgium's capital had gather'd then
Her Beauty and her Chivalry, and bright
The lamps shone o'er fair women and brave men;
A thousand hearts beat happily; and when
Music arose with its voluptuous swell,
Soft eyes look'd love to eyes which spake again,
And all went merry as a marriage bell;
But hush! hark! a deep sound strikes like a rising knell!

Did ye not hear it?—No; 'twas but the wind,
Or the car rattling o'er the stony street;
On with the dance! let joy be unconfined;
No sleep till morn, when Youth and Pleasure meet
To chase the glowing Hours with flying feet—
But hark!—that heavy sound breaks in once more,
As if the clouds its echo would repeat;
And nearer, clearer, deadlier than before!
Arm! Arm! it is—it is—the cannon's opening roar!

Within a window'd niche of that high hall
Sate Brunswick's fated chieftain; he did hear
That sound the first amidst the festival,
And caught its tone with Death's prophetic ear;
And when they smiled because he deem'd it near,
His heart more truly knew that peal too well

S.

11

Which stretch'd his father on a bloody bier,
  And roused the vengeance blood alone could quell;
He rush'd into the field, and, foremost fighting, fell.

Ah! then and there was hurrying to and fro,
  And gathering tears, and tremblings of distress,
And cheeks all pale, which but an hour ago
  Blush'd at the praise of their own loveliness;
  And there were sudden partings, such as press
The life from out young hearts, and choking sighs
  Which ne'er might be repeated; who could guess
  If ever more should meet those mutual eyes,
Since upon night so sweet such awful morn could rise!

And there was mounting in hot haste: the steed,
  The mustering squadron, and the clattering car,
Went pouring forward with impetuous speed,
  And swiftly forming in the ranks of war;
  And the deep thunder peal on peal afar;
And near, the beat of the alarming drum
  Roused up the soldier ere the morning star;
  While throng'd the citizens with terror dumb,
Or whispering, with white lips—"The foe! They come!
    they come!"

And wild and high the "Cameron's gathering" rose!
  The war-note of Lochiel, which Albyn's hills
Have heard, and heard, too, have her Saxon foes:—
  How in the noon of night that pibroch thrills,
  Savage and shrill! But with the breath which fills

Their mountain-pipe, so fill the mountaineers
With the fierce native daring which instils
The stirring memory of a thousand years,
And Evan's, Donald's fame rings in each clansman's ears!

And Ardennes waves above them her green leaves,
Dewy with nature's tear-drops as they pass,
Grieving, if aught inanimate e'er grieves,
Over the unreturning brave,—alas!
Ere evening to be trodden like the grass
Which now beneath them, but above shall grow
In its next verdure, when this fiery mass
Of living valour, rolling on the foe—
And burning with high hope shall moulder cold and low.

Last noon beheld them full of lusty life,
Last eve in Beauty's circle proudly gay,
The midnight brought the signal-sound of strife,
The morn the marshalling in arms,—the day
Battle's magnificently stern array!
The thunder-clouds close o'er it, which when rent,
The earth is cover'd thick with other clay,
Which her own clay shall cover, heap'd and pent,
Rider and horse,—friend, foe,—in one red burial blent!

Byron

19

How sleep the Brave, who sink to Rest,
By all their Country's Wishes blest!
When *Spring*, with dewy Fingers cold,
Returns to deck their hallow'd Mold,
She there shall dress a sweeter Sod,
Than *Fancy's* Feet have ever trod.

By Fairy Hands their Knell is rung,
By Forms unseen their Dirge is sung;
There *Honour* comes, a Pilgrim grey,
To bless the Turf that wraps their Clay,
And *Freedom* shall a-while repair,
To dwell a weeping Hermit there!

William Collins

20

Marching on Tanga, marching the parch'd plain
Of wavering spear-grass past Pangani River,
England came to me—me who had always ta'en
But never given before—England, the giver,
In a vision of three poplar-trees that shiver
On still evenings of summer, after rain,
By Slapton Ley, where reed-beds start and quiver
When scarce a ripple moves the upland grain.
Then I thanked God that now I had suffered pain
And, as the parch'd plain, thirst, and lain awake

Shivering all night through till cold daybreak:
In that I count these sufferings my gain
And her acknowledgment. Nay, more, would fain
Suffer as many more for her sweet sake.

Francis Brett Young

21

After night's thunder far away had rolled
The fiery day had a kernel sweet of cold,
And in the perfect blue the clouds uncurled,
Like the first gods before they made the world
And misery, swimming the stormless sea
In beauty and in divine gaiety.
The smooth white empty road was lightly strewn
With leaves—the holly's Autumn falls in June—
And fir cones standing stiff up in the heat.
The mill-foot water tumbled white and lit
With tossing crystals, happier than any crowd
Of children pouring out of school aloud.
And in the little thickets where a sleeper
For ever might lie lost, the nettle-creeper
And garden warbler sang unceasingly;
While over them shrill shrieked in his fierce glee
The swift with wings and tail as sharp and narrow
As if the bow had flown off with the arrow.
Only the scent of woodbine and hay new-mown
Travelled the road. In the field sloping down,
Park-like, to where its willows showed the brook,
Haymakers rested. The tosser lay forsook

Out in the sun; and the long waggon stood
Without its team, it seemed it never would
Move from the shadow of that single yew.
The team, as still, until their task was due,
Beside the labourers enjoyed the shade
That three squat oaks mid-field together made
Upon a circle of grass and weed uncut,
And on the hollow, once a chalk-pit, but
Now brimmed with nut and elder-flower so clean.
The men leaned on their rakes, about to begin,
But still. And all were silent. All was old,
This morning time, with a great age untold,
Older than Clare and Cobbett, Morland and Crome,
Than, at the field's far edge, the farmer's home,
A white house crouched at the foot of a great tree.
Under the heavens that know not what years be
The men, the beasts, the trees, the implements
Uttered even what they will in times far hence—
All of us gone out of the reach of change—
Immortal in a picture of an old grange.

Edward Thomas

22

Ah! THEN, if mine had been the Painter's hand,
To express what then I saw; and add the gleam,
The light that never was, on sea or land,
The consecration, and the Poet's dream.

Wordsworth

23

It was a bright and cheerful afternoon,
Towards the end of the sunny month of June,
When the north wind congregates in crowds
The floating mountains of the silver clouds
From the horizon—and the stainless sky
Opens beyond them like eternity.
All things rejoiced beneath the sun; the weeds,
The river, and the corn-field, and the reeds;
The willow leaves that glanced in the light breeze,
And the firm foliage of the larger trees.

Shelley

24

Oh! how I love, on a fair summer's eve,
  When streams of light pour down the golden west,
  And on the balmy zephyrs tranquil rest
The silver clouds, far—far away to leave
All meaner thoughts, and take a sweet reprieve
  From little cares; to find, with easy quest,
  A fragrant wild, with Nature's beauty drest,
And there into delight my soul deceive,
There warm my breast with patriotic lore,
  Musing on Milton's fate—on Sidney's bier—
  Till their stern forms before my mind arise:
Perhaps on wing of Poesy upsoar,
  Full often dropping a delicious tear,
  When some melodious sorrow spells mine eyes.

Keats

25

My love is like a red red rose
  That's newly sprung in June:
My love is like the melodie
  That's sweetly play'd in tune.

As fair art thou, my bonnie lass,
  So deep in love am I:
And I will love thee still, my dear,
  Till a' the seas gang dry.

Till a' the seas gang dry, my dear,
  And the rocks melt wi' the sun:
And I will love thee still, my dear,
  While the sands o' life shall run.

And fare thee weel, my only love,
  And fare thee weel awhile!
And I will come again, my love,
  Tho' it were ten thousand mile.

Burns

26

Here's the garden she walked across,
  Arm in my arm, such a short while since:
Hark, now I push its wicket, the moss
  Hinders the hinges, and makes them wince!

She must have reached this shrub ere she turned,
  As back with that murmur the wicket swung;
For she laid the poor snail, my chance foot spurned,
  To feed and forget it the leaves among.

Down this side of the gravel-walk
  She went while her robe's edge brushed the box:
And here she paused in her gracious talk
  To point me a moth on the milk-white phlox.
Roses, ranged in valiant row,
  I will never think that she passed you by!
She loves you noble roses, I know;
  But yonder, see, where the rock plants lie!

This flower she stopped at, finger on lip,
  Stooped over, in doubt, as settling its claim;
Till she gave me, with pride to make no slip,
  Its soft meandering Spanish name:
What a name! Was it love or praise?
  Speech half-asleep, or song half-awake?
I must learn Spanish, one of these days,
  Only for that slow sweet name's sake.

Roses, if I live and do well,
  I may bring her, one of these days,
To fix you fast as fine a spell,
  Fit you each with his Spanish phrase;
But do not detain me now; for she lingers
  There, like sunshine over the ground,
And ever I see her soft white fingers
  Searching after the bud she found.

Flower, you Spaniard, look that you grow not,
    Stay as you are and be loved for ever!
Bud, if I kiss you 'tis that you blow not,
    Mind, the shut pink mouth opens never!
For while thus it pouts, her fingers wrestle,
    Twinkling the audacious leaves between,
Till round they turn and down they nestle—
    Is not the dear mark still to be seen?

Where I find her not, beauties vanish;
    Whither I follow her, beauties flee;
Is there no method to tell her in Spanish
    June's twice June since she breathed it with me?
Come, bud, show me the least of her traces,
    Treasure my lady's lightest footfall!
—Ah, you may flout and turn up your faces—
    Roses, you are not so fair after all!

Robert Browning

27

Of a' the airts the wind can blaw,
    I dearly like the west,
For there the bonnie lassie lives,
    The lassie I lo'e best:
There's wild woods grow, and rivers row,
    And mony a hill between;
But day and night my fancy's flight
    Is ever wi' my Jean.

I see her in the dewy flowers,
  I see her sweet and fair:
I hear her in the tunefu' birds,
  I hear her charm the air:
There's not a bonnie flower that springs
  By fountain, shaw, or green;
There's not a bonnie bird that sings
  But minds me o' my Jean.

Burns

28

Thine eyes still shined for me, though far
  I lonely roved the land or sea:
As I behold yon evening star,
  Which yet beholds not me.

This morn I climbed the misty hill,
  And roamed the pastures through;
How danced thy form before my path
  Amidst the deep-eyed dew!

When the red-bird spread his sable wing,
  And shewed his side of flame;
When the rosebud ripened to the rose,
  In both I read thy name.

R. W. Emerson

29

I thought once how Theocritus had sung
Of the sweet years, the dear and wished-for years,
Who each one in a gracious hand appears
To bear a gift for mortals, old or young:
And, as I mused it in his antique tongue,
I saw, in gradual vision through my tears,
The sweet, sad years, the melancholy years,
Those of my own life, who by turns had flung
A shadow across me. Straightway I was 'ware,
So weeping, how a mystic Shape did move
Behind me, and drew me backward by the hair,
And a voice said in mastery while I strove,...
'Guess now who holds thee?'—'Death,' I said.
    But, there,
The silver answer rang,...'Not Death, but Love.'
E. B. Browning

30

Elizabeth Barrett Browning died June 30, 1861.

O lyric Love, half-angel and half-bird
And all a wonder and a wild desire,—
Boldest of hearts that ever braved the sun,
Took sanctuary within the holier blue,
And sang a kindred soul out to his face,—
Yet human at the red-ripe of the heart—

When the first summons from the darkling earth
Reached thee amid thy chambers, blanched their blue,
And bared them of the glory—to drop down,
To toil for man, to suffer or to die,—
This is the same voice: can thy soul know change?
Hail then, and hearken from the realms of help!
Never may I commence my song, my due
To God who best taught song by gift of thee,
Except with bent head and beseeching hand—
That still, despite the distance and the dark,
What was, again may be; some interchange
Of grace, some splendour once thy very thought,
Some benediction anciently thy smile:
—Never conclude, but raising hand and head
Thither where eyes, that cannot reach, yet yearn
For all hope, all sustainment, all reward,
Their utmost up and on,—so blessing back
In those thy realms of help, that heaven thy home,
Some whiteness which, I judge, thy face makes proud,
Some wanness where, I think, thy foot may fall!

Robert Browning

JULY

THEN came hot *July* boyling like to fire,
That all his garments he had cast away:
Upon a Lyon raging yet with ire
He boldly rode and made him to obay:
It was the beast that whylome did forray
The Nemaean forrest, till th' *Amphytrionide*
Him slew, and with his hide did him array;
Behinde his back a sithe, and by his side
Under his belt he bore a sickle circling wide.

Spenser

July

1

First, *April*, she with mellow showrs
Opens the way for early flowers;
Then after her comes smiling *May*
In a more rich and sweet aray:
Next enters *June*, and brings us more
Jems, than those two, that went before:
Then (lastly) *July* comes, and she
More wealth brings in, then all those three.

Robert Herrick

2

Now the glories of the year
May be viewed at the best,
And the earth doth now appear
In her fairest garments drest.
Sweetly smelling plants and flowers
Do perfume the garden-bowers;
Hill and valley, wood and field,
Mixt with pleasures, profits yield.

Much is found where nothing was,
Herds on every mountain go,
In the meadow flowery grass
Makes both milk and honey flow.
Now each orchard banquets giveth,
Every hedge with fruit relieveth;
And on every shrub and tree
Useful fruits or berries be.

    Walks and ways, which winter marr'd,
By the winds are swept and dried;
    Moorish grounds are now so hard,
That on them we safe may ride.
    Warmth enough the sun doth lend us,
    From his heat the shades defend us;
And thereby we share in these
Safety, profit, pleasure, ease.

    Other blessings, many more,
At this time enjoyèd be;
    And in this my song, therefore,
Praise I give, O Lord, to thee.
    Grant that this my free oblation
    May have gracious acceptation;
And that I may well employ
Every thing, which I enjoy.

George Wither

3

Ask me no more where Jove bestows,
When June is past, the fading rose;
For in your beauty's orient deep
These flowers, as in their causes, sleep.

Ask me no more whither do stray
The golden atoms of the day;
For in pure love heaven did prepare
Those powders to enrich your hair.

July

Ask me no more whither doth haste
The nightingale, when May is past;
For in your sweet dividing throat
She winters, and keeps warm her note.

Ask me no more where those stars light
That downwards fall in dead of night;
For in your eyes they sit, and there
Fixèd become, as in their sphere.

Ask me no more if east or west
The Phoenix builds her spicy nest;
For unto you at last she flies,
And in your fragrant bosom dies.

Thomas Carew

4

O! how much more doth beauty beauteous seem
By that sweet ornament which truth doth give.
The rose looks fair, but fairer we it deem
For that sweet odour which doth in it live.
The canker-blooms have full as deep a dye
As the perfumed tincture of the roses,
Hang on such thorns, and play as wantonly
When summer's breath their masked buds discloses:

But, for their virtue only is their show,
They live unwoo'd, and unrespected fade;
Die to themselves. Sweet roses do not so;
Of their sweet deaths are sweetest odours made:
    And so of you, beauteous and lovely youth,
    When that shall vade, my verse distils your truth.

Shakespeare

5

The rose had been washed, just washed in a shower,
    Which Mary to Anna conveyed,
The plentiful moisture encumbered the flower,
    And weighed down its beautiful head.

The cup was all filled, and the leaves were all wet,
    And it seemed, to a fanciful view,
To weep for the buds it had left with regret
    On the flourishing bush where it grew.

I hastily seized it, unfit as it was
    For a nosegay, so dripping and drowned;
And swinging it rudely, too rudely, alas!
    I snapped it—it fell to the ground.

'And such,' I exclaimed, 'is the pitiless part
    Some act by the delicate mind,
Regardless of wringing and breaking a heart
    Already to sorrow resigned!

'This elegant rose, had I shaken it less,
  Might have bloomed with its owner awhile;
And the tear that is wiped with a little address
  May be followed perhaps by a smile.'

William Cowper

6

It was not in the winter
Our loving lot was cast!
It was the time of roses,
We plucked them as we passed!

That churlish season never frown'd
On early lovers yet!—
Oh no—the world was newly crowned
With flowers, when first we met.

'Twas twilight, and I bade you go,
But still you held me fast;—
It was the time of roses,—
We plucked them as we passed.

Thomas Hood

7

Roses, their sharp spines being gone,
Not royal in their smells alone,
    But in their hue;
Maiden-pinks of odour faint;
Daisies smell-less, yet most quaint,
    And sweet thyme true;

Primrose, first-born child of Ver,
Merry spring-time's harbinger,
  With her bells dim;
Oxlips in their cradles growing,
Marigolds on death-beds blowing,
  Lark-heels trim;

All dear Nature's children sweet
Lie 'fore bride and bridegroom's feet,
  Blessing their sense!
Not an angel of the air,
Bird melodious, or bird fair,
  Be absent hence!

The crow, the slanderous cuckoo, nor
The boding raven, nor chough hoar,
  Nor chattering pie,
May on our bride-house perch or sing,
Or with them any discord bring,
  But from it fly!

Shakespeare or Fletcher

8

Percy Bysshe Shelley drowned, July 8, 1822.

The One remains, they many change and pass;
Heaven's light forever shines, Earth's shadows fly;
Life, like a dome of many-coloured glass,
Stains the white radiance of Eternity,

Until Death tramples it to fragments.—Die,
If thou wouldst be with that which thou dost seek!
Follow where all is fled!—Rome's azure sky,
Flowers, ruins, statues, music, words, are weak
The glory they transfuse with fitting truth to speak.

That Light whose smile kindles the Universe,
That Beauty in which all things work and move,
That Benediction which the eclipsing curse
Of birth can quench not, that sustaining Love
Which through the web of being blindly wove
By man and beast and earth and air and sea,
Burns bright or dim, as each are mirrors of
The fire for which all thirst; now beams on me,
Consuming the last clouds of cold mortality.

The breath whose might I have invoked in song
Descends on me; my spirit's bark is driven,
Far from the shore, far from the trembling throng
Whose sails were never to the tempest given;
The massy earth and spherèd skies are riven!
I am borne darkly, fearfully, afar;
Whilst, burning through the inmost veil of Heaven,
The soul of Adonais, like a star,
Beacons from the abode where the Eternal are.

Shelley

9

Summer has spread a cool, green tent
   Upon the bare poles of this tree;
Where 'tis a joy to sit all day,
   And hear the small birds' melody;
To see the sheep stand bolt upright,
   Nibbling at grass almost their height.

And much I marvel now how men
   Can waste their fleeting days in greed;
That one man should desire more gold
   Than twenty men should truly need;
For is not this green tent more sweet
   Than any chamber of the great?

This tent, at which I spend my day,
   Was made at Nature's cost, not mine;
And when night comes, and I must sleep,
   No matter if my room be fine
Or common, for Content and Health
   Can sleep without the power of Wealth.

W. H. Davies

10

Fresh *fields* and *woods!* the earth's fair *face*,
God's *foot-stool* and man's *dwelling-place.*
I ask not why the first *Believer*
Did love to be a Country liver?

Who to secure pious content
Did pitch by *groves* and *wells* his tent;
Where he might view the boundless *skie*,
And all those glorious *lights* on high:
With flying *meteors, mists,* and *show'rs,*
Subjected *hills, trees, meads,* and *Flow'rs*:
And ev'ry minute bless the King
And wise Creatour of each thing.

   I ask not why he did remove
To happy *Mamre's* holy grove,
Leaving the *Cities* of the plain
To *Lot* and his successless train?
All various Lusts in *Cities* still
Are found; they are the *Thrones* of Ill.
The dismal *Sinks,* where blood is spill'd,
Cages with much uncleanness fill'd.
But *rural shades* are the sweet fense
Of piety and innocence;
They are the *Meek's* calm region, where
Angels descend and rule the sphere:
Where heav'n lies *Leiguer,* and the *Dove*
Duely as *Dew* comes from above.
If *Eden* be on Earth at all
'Tis that which we the *Country* call.

Henry Vaughan

11

Under the greenwood tree,
Who loves to lie with me,
And turn his merry note
Unto the sweet bird's throat,
Come hither, come hither, come hither:
    Here shall he see
    No enemy
But winter and rough weather.

Who doth ambition shun,
And loves to live i' the sun,
Seeking the food he eats,
And pleased with what he gets,
Come hither, come hither, come hither:
    Here shall he see
    No enemy
But winter and rough weather.

Shakespeare

12

I will arise and go now and go to Innisfree,
    And a small cabin build there, of clay and wattles made;
Nine bean rows will I have there, a hive for the honey bee,
    And live alone in the bee-loud glade.

And I shall have some peace there, for peace comes
    dropping slow,
    Dropping from the veils of the morning to where the
      cricket sings;
There midnight's all a glimmer, and noon a purple glow,
    And evening full of the linnets' wings.

I will arise and go now, for always, night and day,
    I hear lake-water lapping with low sounds by the shore;
While I stand on the roadway or on the pavements gray,
    I hear it in the deep heart's core.

                        W. B. Yeats

13

Over here in England I'm helpin' wi' the hay,
    An' I wisht I was in Ireland the livelong day;
Weary on the English hay, an sorra take the wheat!
    Och! Corrymeela an' the blue sky over it.

There's a deep dumb river flowin' by beyont the heavy
    trees,
    This livin' air is moithered wi' the bummin' o' the bees;
I wisht I'd hear the Claddagh burn go runnin' through
    the heat
    Past Corrymeela, wi' the blue sky over it.

The people that's in England is richer nor the Jews,
    There's not the smallest young gossoon but thravels in
    his shoes!
I'd give the pipe between me teeth to see a barefut child,
    Och! Corrymeela and the low south wind.

Here's hands so full o' money an' hearts so full o' care,
　By the luck o' love! I'd still go light for all I did go bare.
'God save ye, *colleen dhas*,' I said: the girl she thought
　　me wild.
　Far Corrymeela, an' the low south wind.

D'ye mind me now, the song at night is mortial hard to
　　raise,
　The girls are heavy goin' here, the boys are ill to plase;
When onest I'm out this workin' hive, 'tis I'll be back
　　again—
　Ay, Corrymeela, in the same soft rain.

The puff o' smoke from one ould roof before an English
　　town!
　For a *shaugh* wid Andy Feelan here I'd give a silver
　　crown,
For a curl o' hair like Mollie's ye'll ask the like in vain,
　Sweet Corrymeela, an' the same soft rain.

Moira O'Neill

14

　To one who has been long in city pent,
　　'Tis very sweet to look into the fair
　　And open face of heaven,—to breath a prayer
　Full in the smile of the blue firmament.
　Who is more happy, when, with heart's content,
　　Fatigued he sinks into some pleasant lair
　　Of wavy grass, and reads a debonair

And gentle tale of love and languishment?
Returning home at evening, with an ear
   Catching the notes of Philomel,—an eye
Watching the sailing cloudlet's bright career,
   He mourns that day so soon has glided by:
E'en like the passage of an angel's tear
   That falls through the clear ether silently.

Keats

15

Oh! I could tarry under these green boughs,
In these soft shadows, all the Summer long,
If only one sweet Nymph with sunny brows
Would teach me all her ancient woodland song,
Till I had learn'd such pure and simple breath
As pour'd into the dusty ears of kings
Would make them thirsty for a wild-rose wreath,
Green glens, and thymy slopes, and pure cold rills.

Frederick Tennyson

16

I never prayed for Dryads, to haunt the woods again;
More welcome were the presence of hungering, thirsting
    men,
Whose doubts we could unravel, whose hopes we could fulfil,
Our wisdom tracing backward, the river to the rill;
Were such beloved forerunners one summer day restored,
Then, then we might discover the Muse's mystic hoard.

Oh, dear divine Comatas, I would that thou and I
Beneath this broken sunlight this leisure day might lie;
Where trees from distant forests, whose names were strange
    to thee,
Should bend their amorous branches within thy reach to be,
And flowers thine Hellas knew not, which art hath made
    more fair,
Should shed their shining petals upon thy fragrant hair.

Then thou shouldst calmly listen with ever-changing looks
To songs of younger minstrels and plots of modern books,
And wonder at the daring of poets later born,
Whose thoughts are unto thy thoughts as noon-tide is to morn;
And little shouldst thou grudge them their greater strength
    of soul,
Thy partners in the torch-race, though nearer to the goal.

As when ancestral portraits look gravely from the walls
Upon the youthful baron who treads their echoing halls;
And whilst he builds new turrets, the thrice ennobled heir
Would gladly wake his grandsire his home and feast to share;
So from Ægean laurels that hide thine ancient urn
I fain would call thee hither, my sweeter lore to learn.

Or in thy cedarn prison thou waitest for the bee:
Ah, leave that simple honey, and take thy food from me.
My sun is stooping westward. Entrancèd dreamer, haste:
There's fruitage in my garden, that I would have thee taste.
Now lift the lid a moment: now, Dorian shepherd, speak:
Two minds shall flow together, the English and the Greek.
                             W. J. Cory

17

When I am living in the Midlands
  That are sodden and unkind,
I light my lamp in the evening:
  My work is left behind;
And the great hills of the South Country
  Come back into my mind.

The great hills of the South Country
  They stand along the sea:
And it's there walking in the high woods
  That I could wish to be,
And the men that were boys when I was a boy
  Walking along with me.

The men that live in North England
  I saw them for a day:
Their hearts are set upon the waste falls,
  Their skies are fast and grey:
From their castle-walls a man may see
  The mountains far away.

The men that live in West England
  They see the Severn strong,
A-rolling on rough water brown
  Light aspen leaves along.
They have the secret of the Rocks,
  And the oldest kind of song.

But the men that live in the South Country
   Are the kindest and most wise,
They get their laughter from the loud surf
   And the faith in their happy eyes
Comes surely from our Sister the Spring
   When over the sea she flies;
The violets suddenly bloom at her feet,
   She blesses us with surprise.

I never get between the pines
   But I smell the Sussex air,
Nor I never come on a belt of sand
   But the old place is there.
And along the sky the line of the downs
   So noble and so bare.

A lost thing could I never find,
   Nor a broken thing mend:
And I fear I shall be all alone
   When I get towards the end.
Who will there be to comfort me
   Or who will be my friend?

I will gather and carefully make my friends
   Of the men of the Sussex Weald.
They watch the stars from distant folds,
   They stiffly plough the field.
By them and the God of the South Country
   My poor soul shall be healed.

If I ever become a rich man,
  Or if ever I grow to be old,
I will build a house with deep thatch
  To shelter me from the cold,
And there shall the Sussex songs be sung
  And the story of Sussex told.

I will hold my house in the high wood
  Within a walk of the sea,
And the men that were boys when I was a boy
  Shall sit and drink with me.

Hilaire Belloc

18

When to the sessions of sweet silent thought
I summon up remembrance of things past,
I sigh the lack of many a thing I sought,
And with old woes new wail my dear times' waste:
Then can I drown an eye, unus'd to flow,
For precious friends hid in death's dateless night,
And weep afresh love's long since cancell'd woe,
And moan the expense of many a vanish'd sight:
Then can I grieve at grievances foregone,
And heavily from woe to woe tell o'er
The sad account of fore-bemoaned moan,
Which I new pay as if not paid before.
  But if the while I think on thee, dear friend,
  All losses are restor'd, and sorrows end.

Shakespeare

19

Night sank upon the dusky beach, and on the purple sea,
Such night in England ne'er had been, nor e'er again shall
be.
From Eddystone to Berwick bounds, from Lynn to Mil-
ford Bay,
That time of slumber was as bright and busy as the day;
For swift to east and swift to west the ghastly war-flame
spread,
High on St Michael's Mount it shone: it shone on Beachy
Head.
Far on the deep the Spaniard saw, along each southern
shire,
Cape beyond cape, in endless range, those twinkling points
of fire.
The fisher left his skiff to rock on Tamar's glittering
waves:
The rugged miners poured to war from Mendip's sunless
caves:
O'er Longleat's towers, o'er Cranbourne's oaks, the fiery
herald flew:
He roused the shepherds of Stonehenge, the rangers of
Beaulieu.
Right sharp and quick the bells all night rang out from
Bristol town,
And ere the day three hundred horse had met on Clifton
down;

The sentinel on Whitehall gate looked forth into the
  night,
And saw o'erhanging Richmond Hill the streak of blood-
  red light,
Then bugle's note and cannon's roar the deathlike silence
  broke,
And with one start, and with one cry, the royal city woke.
At once on all her stately gates arose the answering fires;
At once the wild alarum clashed from all her reeling
  spires;
From all the batteries of the Tower pealed loud the voice
  of fear;
And all the thousand masts of Thames sent back a louder
  cheer;
And from the furthest wards was heard the rush of hurrying
  feet,
And the broad streams of pikes and flags rushed down each
  roaring street;
And broader still became the blaze, and louder still the din,
As fast from every village round the horse came spurring
  in:
And eastward straight from wild Blackheath the warlike
  errand went,
And roused in many an ancient hall the gallant squires of
  Kent.
Southward from Surrey's pleasant hills flew those bright
  couriers forth;
High on bleak Hampstead's swarthy moor they started for
  the north;

And on, and on, without a pause, untired they bounded
    still:

All night from tower to tower they sprang; they sprang
    from hill to hill:

Till the proud peak unfurled the flag o'er Darwin's rocky
    dales,

Till like volcanoes flared to heaven the stormy hills of
    Wales,

Till twelve fair counties saw the blaze on Malvern's lonely
    height,

Till streamed in crimson on the wind the Wrekin's crest
    of light,

Till broad and fierce the star came forth on Ely's stately
    fane,

And tower and hamlet rose in arms o'er all the boundless
    plain;

Till Belvoir's lordly terraces the sign to Lincoln sent,

And Lincoln sped the message on o'er the wide vale of
    Trent;

Till Skiddaw saw the fire that burned on Gaunt's em-
    battled pile,

And the red glare on Skiddaw roused the burghers of
    Carlisle.

Lord Macaulay

20

I stood tip-toe upon a little hill,
The air was cooling, and so very still,
That the sweet buds which with a modest pride
Pull droopingly, in slanting curve aside,
Their scantly-leaved, and finely-tapering stems,
Had not yet lost their starry diadems
Caught from the early sobbing of the morn.
The clouds were pure and white as flocks new-shorn,
And fresh from the clear brook; sweetly they slept
On the blue fields of heaven, and then there crept
A little noiseless noise among the leaves,
Born of the very sigh that silence heaves:
For not the faintest motion could be seen
Of all the shades that slanted o'er the green.

Keats

21

Robert Burns died July 21, 1796.

What woos the world to yonder shrine?
What sacred day, what dust divine?
Was this some Master faultless-fine,
      In whom we praise
The cunning of the jewelled line
      And carven phrase?

A searcher of our source and goal,
A reader of God's secret scroll?
A Shakespeare, flashing o'er the whole
 Of man's domain
The splendour of his cloudless soul
 And perfect brain?

Some Keats, to Grecian gods allied,
Clasping all beauty as his bride?
Some Shelley, soaring dim-descried
 Above Time's throng,
And heavenward hurling wild and wide
 His spear of song?

A lonely Wordsworth, from the crowd
Half hid in light, half veiled in cloud?
A sphere-born Milton, cold and proud,
 In hallowing dews
Dipt, and with gorgeous ritual vowed
 Unto the Muse?

Nay, none of these,—and little skilled
On heavenly heights to sing and build!
Thine, thine, O Earth, whose fields he tilled,
 And thine alone,
Was he whose fiery heart lies stilled
 'Neath yonder stone.

  . . . . .

No mystic torch through Time he bore,
No virgin veil from Life he tore;

July

His soul no bright insignia wore
    Of starry birth;
He saw what all men see—no more—
    In heaven and earth:

But as, when thunder crashes nigh,
All darkness opes one flaming eye,
And the world leaps against the sky,—
    So fiery-clear
Did the old truths that we pass by
    To him appear.

William Watson

22

How the blithe lark runs up the golden stair
That leans thro' cloudy gates from heaven to earth,
And all alone in the empyreal air
Fills it with jubilant sweet songs of mirth;
How far he seems, how far
With the light upon his wings,
Is it a bird, or star
That shines, and sings?

What matter if the days be dark and frore,
That sunbeam tells of other days to be,
And singing in the light that floods him o'er
In joy he overtakes Futurity;

Under cloud-arches vast
He peeps, and sees behind
Great Summer coming fast
Adown the wind!

And now he dives into a rainbow's rivers,
In streams of gold and purple he is drown'd,
Shrilly the arrows of his song he shivers,
As tho' the stormy drops were turn'd to sound;
And now he issues thro',
He scales a cloudy tower,
Faintly, like falling dew,
His fast notes shower.

Let every wind be hush'd, that I may hear
The wondrous things he tells the World below,
Things that we dream of he is watching near,
Hopes, that we never dream'd, he would bestow;
Alas! the storm hath roll'd
Back the gold gates again,
Or surely he had told
All Heaven to men!

So the victorious Poet sings alone,
And fills with light his solitary home,
And thro' that glory sees new worlds foreshown,
And hears high songs, and triumphs yet to come;
He waves the air of Time
With thrills of golden chords,
And makes the world to climb
On linked words.

July

What if his hair be gray, his eye be dim,
If wealth forsake him, and if friends be cold,
Wonder unbars her thousand gates to him,
Truth never fails, nor Beauty waxeth old;
More than he tells his eyes
Behold, his spirit hears,
Of grief, and joy, and sighs
'Twixt joy and tears.

Blest is the man who with the sound of song
Can charm away the heartache, and forget
The frost of Penury, and the stings of Wrong,
And drown the fatal whisper of Regret;
Darker are the abodes
Of Kings, though his be poor,
While Fancies, like the Gods,
Pass through his door.

Singing thou scalest Heaven upon thy wings,
Thou liftest a glad heart into the skies;
He maketh his own sunrise, while he sings,
And turns the dusty earth to Paradise;
I see thee sail along
Far up the sunny streams;
Unseen, I hear his song,
I see his dreams.

Frederick Tennyson

23

But who is He, with modest looks,
And clad in homely russet brown?
He murmurs near the running brooks
A music sweeter than their own.

He is retired as noontide dew,
Or fountain in a noon-day grove;
And you must love him, ere to you
He will seem worthy of your love.

The outward shows of sky and earth,
Of hill and valley, he has viewed;
And impulses of deeper birth
Have come to him in solitude.

In common things that round us lie
Some random truths he can impart,—
The harvest of a quiet eye
That broods and sleeps on his own heart.

But he is weak; both Man and Boy,
Hath been an idler in the land;
Contented if he might enjoy
The things which others understand.

—Come hither in thy hour of strength;
Come, weak as is a breaking wave!
Here stretch thy body at full length;
Or build thy house upon this grave.

Wordsworth

July

24

A Paradise on earth is found,
Though far from vulgar sight,
Which with those pleasures doth abound
That it Elysium hight,

Where, in delights that never fade,
The Muses lullèd be,
And sit at pleasure in the shade
Of many a stately tree,

Which no rough tempest makes to reel,
Nor their strait bodies bows,
Their lofty tops do never feel
The weight of winter's snows;

In groves that evermore are green,
No falling leaf is there,
But Philomel (of birds the queen)
In musick spends the year.

The merl upon her myrtle perch
There to the mavis sings,
Who from the top of some curl'd berch
Those notes redoubled rings;

The winter here a summer is,
No waste is made by time,
Nor doth the autumn ever miss
The blossoms of the prime.

There in perpetual summer's shade,
Apollo's prophets sit,
Among the flowers that never fade,
But flourish like their wit.

Decay nor age there nothing knows,
There is continual youth,
As time on plant or creatures grows,
So still their strength renew'th.

The poets paradise this is,
To which but few can come;
The Muses only bower of bliss,
Their dear Elysium.

Michael Drayton

25

Samuel Taylor Coleridge died July 25, 1834.

Ye Clouds! that far above me float and pause,
 Whose pathless march no mortal may controul!
 Ye Ocean-Waves! that, wheresoe'er ye roll,
Yield homage only to eternal laws!
Ye Woods! that listen to the night-birds singing,
 Midway the smooth and perilous slope reclined,
Save when your own imperious branches swinging,
 Have made a solemn music of the wind!
Where, like a man beloved of God,
Through glooms, which never woodman trod,
 How oft, pursuing fancies holy,
My moonlight way o'er flowering weeds I wound,
 Inspired, beyond the guess of folly,

By each rude shape and wild unconquerable sound!
O ye loud Waves! and O ye Forests high!
  And O ye Clouds that far above me soared!
Thou rising Sun! thou blue rejoicing sky!
  Yea, every thing that is and will be free!
  Bear witness for me, wheresoe'er ye be,
  With what deep worship I have still adored
    The spirit of divinest Liberty.

S. T. Coleridge

26

A Sensitive Plant in a garden grew,
And the young winds fed it with silver dew,
And it opened its fan-like leaves to the light,
And closed them beneath the kisses of Night.

And the Spring arose on the garden fair,
Like the Spirit of Love felt everywhere;
And each flower and herb on Earth's dark breast
Rose from the dreams of its wintry rest.

But none ever trembled and panted with bliss
In the garden, the field, or the wilderness,
Like a doe in the noon-tide with love's sweet want,
As the companionless Sensitive Plant.

The snowdrop, and then the violet,
Arose from the ground with warm rain wet,
And their breath was mixed with fresh odour, sent
From the turf, like the voice and the instrument.

Then the pied wind-flowers and the tulip tall,
And narcissi, the fairest among them all,
Who gaze on their eyes in the stream's recess,
Till they die of their own dear loveliness;

And the Naiad-like lily of the vale,
Whom youth makes so fair and passion so pale
That the light of its tremulous bells is seen
Through their pavilions of tender green;

And the hyacinth purple, and white, and blue,
Which flung from its bells a sweet peal anew
Of music so delicate, soft, and intense,
It was felt like an odour within the sense;

And the rose like a nymph to the bath addressed,
Which unveiled the depth of her glowing breast,
Till, fold after fold, to the fainting air
The soul of her beauty and love lay bare:

And the wand-like lily, which lifted up,
As a Mænad, its moonlight-coloured cup,
Till the fiery star, which is its eye,
Gazed through the clear dew on the tender sky;

And the jessamine faint, and the sweet tuberose,
The sweetest flower for scent that blows;
And all rare blossoms from every clime
Grew in that garden in perfect prime.

And on the stream whose inconstant bosom
Was pranked, under boughs of embowering blossom,
With golden and green light, slanting through
Their heaven of many a tangled hue,

Broad water-lilies lay tremulously,
And starry river-buds glimmered by,
And around them the soft stream did glide and dance
With a motion of sweet sound and radiance.

And the sinuous paths of lawn and of moss,
Which led through the garden along and across,
Some open at once to the sun and the breeze,
Some lost among bowers of blossoming trees,

Were all paved with daisies and delicate bells
As fair as the fabulous asphodels,
And flow'rets which, drooping as day drooped too,
Fell into pavilions, white, purple, and blue,
To roof the glow-worm from the evening dew.

And from this undefilèd Paradise
The flowers (as an infant's awakening eyes
Smile on its mother, whose singing sweet
Can first lull, and at last must awaken it),

When Heaven's blithe winds had unfolded them,
As mine-lamps enkindle a hidden gem,
Shone smiling to Heaven, and every one
Shared joy in the light of the gentle sun;

For each one was interpenetrated
With the light and the odour its neighbour shed,
Like young lovers whom youth and love make dear,
Wrapped and filled by their mutual atmosphere.

But the Sensitive Plant which could give small fruit
Of the love which it felt from the leaf to the root,
Received more than all, it loved more than ever,
Where none wanted but it, could belong to the giver,—

For the Sensitive Plant has no bright flower;
Radiance and odour are not its dower;
It loves, even like Love, its deep heart is full,
It desires what it has not, the Beautiful!

The light winds which from unsustaining wings
Shed the music of many murmurings;
The beams which dart from many a star
Of the flowers whose hues they bear afar;

The plumèd insects swift and free,
Like golden boats on a sunny sea,
Laden with light and odour, which pass
Over the gleam of the living grass;

The unseen clouds of the dew, which lie
Like fire in the flowers till the sun rides high,
Then wander like spirits among the spheres,
Each cloud faint with the fragrance it bears;

July

The quivering vapours of dim noontide,
Which like a sea o'er the warm earth glide,
In which every sound, and odour, and beam,
Move, as reeds in a single stream;

Each and all like ministering angels were
For the Sensitive Plant sweet joy to bear,
Whilst the lagging hours of the day went by
Like windless clouds o'er a tender sky.

And when evening descended from Heaven above,
And the Earth was all rest, and the air was all love,
And delight, though less bright, was far more deep,
And the day's veil fell from the world of sleep,

And the beasts, and the birds, and the insects were
    drowned
In an ocean of dreams without a sound;
Whose waves never mark, though they ever impress
The light sand which paves it, consciousness;

(Only overhead the sweet nightingale
Ever sang more sweet as the day might fail,
And snatches of its Elysian chant
Were mixed with the dreams of the Sensitive Plant);–

The Sensitive Plant was the earliest
Upgathered into the bosom of rest;
A sweet child weary of its delight,
The feeblest and yet the favourite,
Cradled within the embrace of Night.

Shelley

27

There was a Power in this sweet place,
An Eve in this Eden; a ruling grace
Which to the flowers, did they waken or dream,
Was as God is to the starry scheme.

A Lady, the wonder of her kind,
Whose form was upborne by a lovely mind
Which, dilating, had moulded her mien and motion
Like a sea-flower unfolded beneath the ocean,

Tended the garden from morn to even:
And the meteors of that sublunar Heaven,
Like the lamps of the air when Night walks forth,
Laughed round her footsteps up from the Earth!

She had no companion of mortal race,
But her tremulous breath and her flushing face
Told, whilst the morn kissed the sleep from her eyes,
That her dreams were less slumber than Paradise:

As if some bright Spirit for her sweet sake
Had deserted Heaven while the stars were awake,
As if yet around her he lingering were,
Though the veil of daylight concealed him from her.

Her step seemed to pity the grass it pressed;
You might hear, by the heaving of her breast,
That the coming and going of the wind
Brought pleasure there and left passion behind.

And wherever her aëry footstep trod,
Her trailing hair from the grassy sod
Erased its light vestige, with shadowy sweep,
Like a sunny storm o'er the dark green deep.

I doubt not the flowers of that garden sweet
Rejoiced in the sound of her gentle feet;
I doubt not they felt the spirit that came
From her glowing fingers through all their frame.

She sprinkled bright water from the stream
On those that were faint with the sunny beam;
And out of the cups of the heavy flowers
She emptied the rain of the thunder-showers.

She lifted their heads with her tender hands,
And sustained them with rods and osier-bands;
If the flowers had been her own infants, she
Could never have nursed them more tenderly.

And all killing insects and gnawing worms,
And things of obscene and unlovely forms,
She bore, in a basket of Indian woof,
Into the rough woods far aloof,—

In a basket, of grasses and wild-flowers full,
The freshest her gentle hands could pull
For the poor banished insects, whose intent,
Although they did ill, was innocent.

But the bee and the beamlike ephemeris
Whose path is the lightning's, and soft moths that kiss
The sweet lips of the flowers, and harm not, did she
Make her attendant angels be.

And many an antenatal tomb,
Where butterflies dream of the life to come,
She left clinging round the smooth and dark
Edge of the odorous cedar bark.

This fairest creature from earliest Spring
Thus moved through the garden ministering
All the sweet season of Summertide,
And ere the first leaf looked brown—she died!

Shelley

28

I love to peep out on a summer's morn,
    Just as the scouting rabbit seeks her shed,
And the coy hare squats nestling in the corn,
    Frit at the bow'd ear tott'ring o'er her head;
And blund'ring pheasant, that from covert springs,
    His short sleep broke by early trampling feet,
Makes one to startle with his rustling wings,
    As through the boughs he seeks more safe retreat.
The little flower, begemm'd around with drops
    That shine at sunrise like to burnish'd gold,

July

'Tis sweet to view: the milkmaid often stops,
  And wonders much such spangles to behold;
The hedger, too, admires them deck the thorn,—
  And thinks he sees no beauties like the Morn.

John Clare

29

I am this Fountain's God; below
My Waters to a River grow,
And 'twixt two Banks with Osiers set,
That only prosper in the Wet,
Through the Meadows do they glide,
Wheeling still on ev'ry Side,
Sometimes winding round about,
To find the even'st Channel out.
And if thou wilt go with me
Leaving mortal Company,
In the cool Streams shalt thou lye,
Free from harm as well as I:
I will give thee for thy Food,
No Fish that useth in the Mud,
But Trout and Pike that love to swim
Where the Gravel from the Brim,
Through the pure Streams may be seen:
Orient Pearl fit for a Queen,
Will I give thy Love to win,
And a Shell to keep them in:

Not a Fish in all my Brook
That shall disobey thy Look,
But when thou wilt, come sliding by,
And from thy white Hand take a Fly.
And to make thee understand,
How I can my Waves command,
They shall bubble whilst I sing
Sweeter than the Silver Spring.

THE SONG

Do not fear to put thy Feet
Naked in the River sweet;
Think not Leech, or Newt, or Toad,
Will bite thy Foot, when thou hast trod;
Nor let the Water rising high,
As thou wads't in, make thee cry
And sob, but ever live with me,
And not a Wave shall trouble thee.

John Fletcher

30

The copse ha' got his sheädy boughs;
  Wi' blackbirds' evenen whissles;
The hills ha' sheep upon ther brows,
  The zummerleäze ha' thissles.
The meäds be gay in grassy May,
  But O vrom hill to holler,
Let I look down upon a groun'
  O' carn a-turnen yoller.

An' pease da grow in tangled beds,
　　An' beäns be sweet to snuff, O;
The tiaper woats da bend their heads,
　　The barley's beard is rough, O;
The turnip green is fresh between
　　The carn in hill ar holler,
But I'd look down upon the groun'
　　O' wheat a-turnen yoller.

'Tis merry when the brawny men
　　Da come to reap it down, O,
Wher glossy red the poppy head
　　'S among the sta'ks so brown, O;
'Tis merry while the wheat's in pile
　　Ar when, by hill ar holler,
The leäzers thick da stoop to pick
　　The ears so ripe an' yoller.

William Barnes

31

Great purple clouds in the western sky,
　　Hung thick o'er a blaze of golden white,
And below that glory there seems to lie,
　　A cushion of silver: not so bright
But it dulls to a grey that entombs the day
　　And heralds the march of night.

One tree hides a third of the gorgeous west,—
  A disk of black is its dusky growth—
Yet not hides: nay perhaps displays at best
  Through the chinks which it opens nothing loth:
While its outline bold cuts silver and gold,
  And heightens the blaze of both.

And up to the glory of golden white,
  With the purple above and the silver below,
There's a river lane that is darkly bright,
  Softly and smoothly and quietly aglow,
Blue willows beside it, night hasting to hide it,
  Day sorry to let it go.

The tree grows blacker, the night falls fast,
  And purple and silver and white must fade:
But something was shown us which can't but last:
  Has a song been sung? has a play been played?
Has a lesson been taught, or was all for naught?
  Well—nothing endures like the past.

                                        J. K. Stephen

AUGUST

THE sixt was *August*, being rich arrayd
  In garment all of gold downe to the ground;
  Yet rode he not, but led a lovely Mayd
  Forth by the lilly hand, the which was cround
  With eares of corne, and full her hand was found;
  That was the righteous Virgin, which of old
  Liv'd here on earth, and plenty made abound;
  But after Wrong was lov'd, and Justice solde,
She left th' unrighteous world and was to heaven
    extold.

                                    Spenser

August

I

THE stars burnt out in the pale blue air,
And the thin white moon lay withering there;
To tower, and cavern, and rift, and tree,
The owl and the bat fled drowsily.
Day had kindled the dewy woods,
 And the rocks above and the stream below,
And the vapours in their multitudes,
 And the Apennines' shroud of summer snow,
And clothed with light of aëry gold
The mists in their eastern caves uprolled.

Day had awakened all things that be,
The lark and the thrush and the swallow free,
 And the milkmaid's song and the mower's scythe,
And the matin-bell and the mountain bee:
Fireflies were quenched on the dewy corn,
 Glow-worms went out on the river's brim,
 Like lamps which a student forgets to trim:
The beetle forgot to wind his horn,
 The crickets were still in the meadow and hill:
Like a flock of rooks at a farmer's gun
Night's dreams and terrors, every one,
Fled from the brains which are their prey
From the lamp's death to the morning ray.

All rose to do the task He set to each,
 Who shaped us to His ends and not our own;
The million rose to learn, and one to teach
 What none yet ever knew or can be known.

Shelley

2

How sweet the moonlight sleeps upon this bank!
Here will we sit, and let the sounds of music
Creep in our ears: soft stillness and the night
Become the touches of sweet harmony.
Sit, Jessica: look, how the floor of heaven
Is thick inlaid with patines of bright gold:
There's not the smallest orb, which thou behold'st
But in his motion like an angel sings,
Still quiring to the young-eyed cherubins;
Such harmony is in immortal souls;
But whilst this muddy vesture of decay
Doth grossly close it in, we cannot hear it.

Shakespeare

3

Earth has not anything to show more fair:
Dull would he be of soul who could pass by
A sight so touching in its majesty:
This City now doth, like a garment, wear
The beauty of the morning; silent, bare,
Ships, towers, domes, theatres, and temples lie
Open unto the fields, and to the sky;
All bright and glittering in the smokeless air
Never did sun more beautifully steep
In his first splendour, valley, rock, or hill

Ne'er saw I, never felt, a calm so deep!
The river glideth at his own sweet will:
Dear God! the very houses seem asleep;
And all that mighty heart is lying still!
Wordsworth

4

What of the faith and fire within us
　　Men who march away
　　Ere the barn-cocks say
　　Night is growing gray,
To hazards whence no tears can win us;
What of the faith and fire within us
　　Men who march away?

Is it a purblind prank, O think you,
　　Friend with the musing eye,
　　Who watch us stepping by
　　With doubt and dolorous sigh?
Can much pondering so hoodwink you!
Is it a purblind prank, O think you,
　　Friend with the musing eye?

Nay. We well see what we are doing,
　　Though some may not see—
　　Dalliers as they be—
　　England's need are we;
Her distress would leave us rueing:
Nay. We well see what we are doing,
　　Though some may not see!

In our heart of hearts believing
    Victory crowns the just,
    And that braggarts must
    Surely bite the dust,
Press we to the field ungrieving,
In our heart of hearts believing
    Victory crowns the just.

Hence the faith and fire within us
    Men who march away
    Ere the barn-cocks say
    Night is growing gray,
To hazards whence no tears can win us;
Hence the faith and fire within us
    Men who march away.

(1914)   *Thomas Hardy*

5

    Rise up, rise up,
    And, as the trumpet blowing
    Chases the dreams of men,
    As the dawn glowing
    The stars that left unlit
    The land and water,
    Rise up and scatter
    The dew that covers
    The print of last night's lovers—
    Scatter it, scatter it!

August

While you are listening
To the clear horn,
Forget, men, everything
On this earth newborn,
Except that it is lovelier
Than any mysteries.
Open your eyes to the air
That has washed the eyes of the stars
Through all the dewy night:
Up with the light,
To the old wars;
Arise, arise!

Edward Thomas

6

For the last time, may be, upon the knoll
I stand. The eve is golden, languid, sad,...
Day like a tragic actor plays his rôle
To the last whispered word, and falls gold-clad.
I, too, take leave of all I ever had.

They shall not say I went with heavy heart:
Heavy I am, but soon I shall be free;
I love them all, but O I now depart
A little sadly, strangely, fearfully,
As one who goes to try a Mystery.

August

The bell is sounding down in Dedham Vale:
Be still, O bell! too often standing here
When all the air was tremulous, fine, and pale,
Thy golden note so calm, so still, so clear,
Out of my stony heart has struck a tear.

And now tears are not mine. I have release
From all the former and the later pain;
Like the mid-sea I rock in boundless peace,
Soothed by the charity of the deep sea rain....
Calm rain! Calm sea! Calm found, long sought in
      vain.

O bronzen pines, evening of gold and blue,
Steep mellow slope, brimmed twilit pools below,
Hushed trees, still vale dissolving in the dew,
Farewell! Farewell! There is no more to do.
We have been happy. Happy now I go.

                                            Robert Nichols

7

With proud thanksgiving, a mother for her children,
England mourns for her dead across the sea.
Flesh of her flesh they were, spirit of her spirit,
Fallen in the cause of the free.

Solemn the drums thrill: Death august and royal
Sings sorrow up into immortal spheres.
There is music in the midst of desolation
And a glory that shines upon our tears.

They went with songs to the battle, they were young,
Straight of limb, true of eye, steady and aglow.
They were staunch to the end against odds uncounted,
They fell with their faces to the foe.

They shall grow not old, as we that are left grow old:
Age shall not weary them, nor the years condemn.
At the going down of the sun and in the morning
We will remember them.

They mingle not with their laughing comrades again;
They sit no more at familiar tables of home;
They have no lot in our labour of the day-time;
They sleep beyond England's foam.

But where our desires are and our hopes profound,
Felt as a well-spring that is hidden from sight,
To the innermost heart of their own land they are known
As the stars are known to the Night;

As the stars that shall be bright when we are dust
Moving in marches upon the heavenly plain,
As the stars that are starry in the time of our darkness,
To the end, to the end, they remain.

Laurence Binyon

8

Look forth!—that Stream behold,
THAT STREAM upon whose bosom we have passed
Floating at ease while nations have effaced
Nations, and Death has gathered to his fold
Long lines of mighty Kings—look forth, my Soul!

(Nor in this vision be thou slow to trust)
The living Waters, less and less by guilt
Stained and polluted, brighten as they roll,
Till they have reached the eternal City—built
For the perfècted Spirits of the just!

Wordsworth

9

Clear had the day been from the dawn,
All chequer'd was the sky,
The clouds like scarfs of cobweb lawn
Veil'd heaven's most glorious eye.
The wind had no more strength than this,
That leisurely it blew,
To make one leaf the next to kiss
That closely by it grew.
The rills, that on the pebbles play'd,
Might now be heard at will;
This world they only musick made,
Else every thing was still.
The flowers like brave embroider'd girls,
Look'd as they most desir'd
To see whose head with orient pearls
Most curiously was tyr'd;
And to it self the subtil air
Such sovereignty assumes,
That it receiv'd too large a share
From nature's rich perfumes.

Michael Drayton

10

The tedded hay, the first fruits of the soil,
The tedded hay and corn-sheaves in one field,
Show summer gone, ere come. The foxglove tall
Sheds its loose purple bells, or in the gust,
Or when it bends beneath the up-springing lark,
Or mountain-finch alighting. And the rose
(In vain the darling of successful love)
Stands, like some boasted beauty of past years,
The thorns remaining, and the flowers all gone.
Nor can I find, amid my lonely walk
By rivulet, or spring, or wet road-side,
That blue and bright-eyed floweret of the brook,
Hope's gentle gem, the sweet Forget-me-not!

S. T. Coleridge

11

When my mother died I was very young,
And my father sold me while yet my tongue
Could scarcely cry "'weep! 'weep! 'weep! 'weep!'
So your chimneys I sweep, and in soot I sleep.

There's little Tom Dacre, who cried when his head,
That curl'd like a lamb's back, was shav'd: so I said
'Hush, Tom! never mind it, for when your head's bare
You know that the soot cannot spoil your white hair.'

And so he was quiet, and that very night,
As Tom was a-sleeping, he had such a sight!—
That thousands of sweepers, Dick, Joe, Ned, and Jack,
Were all of them locked up in coffins of black.

And by came an Angel who had a bright key,
And he open'd the coffins and set them all free;
Then down a green plain leaping, laughing, they run,
And wash in a river, and shine in the sun.

Then naked and white, all their bags left behind,
They rise upon clouds and sport in the wind;
And the Angel told Tom, if he'd be a good boy,
He'd have God for his father, and never want joy.

And so Tom awoke; and we rose in the dark,
And got with our bags and our brushes to work.
Tho' the morning was cold, Tom was happy and warm;
So if all do their duty they need not fear harm.

William Blake

Lord Shaftesbury's Chimney-sweeper's Bill became law August 11, 1875.

12

William Blake died August 12, 1827.

Bring me my bow of burning gold!
Bring me my arrows of desire!
Bring me my spear! O clouds, unfold!
Bring me my chariot of fire!

I will not cease from mental fight,
   Nor shall my sword sleep in my hand,
Till we have built Jerusalem
   In England's green and pleasant land.

                         William Blake

13

My mother bore me in the southern wild,
   And I am black, but O! my soul is white;
White as an angel is the English child,
   But I am black, as if bereav'd of light.

My mother taught me underneath a tree,
   And, sitting down before the heat of day,
She took me on her lap and kissèd me,
   And, pointing to the east, began to say:

'Look on the rising sun,—there God does live,
   And gives His light and gives His heat away;
And flowers and trees and beasts and men receive
   Comfort in morning, joy in the noonday.

'And we are put on earth a little space,
   That we may learn to bear the beams of love;
And these black bodies and this sunburnt face
   Are but a cloud, and like a shady grove.

'For when our souls have learn'd the heat to bear,
   The cloud will vanish; we shall hear His voice,
Saying: "Come out from the grove, My love and
     care,
   And round My golden tent like lambs rejoice."'

Thus did my mother say, and kissèd me;
  And thus I say to little English boy.
When I from black, and he from white cloud free,
  And round the tent of God like lambs we joy,

I'll shade him from the heat, till he can bear
  To lean in joy upon our Father's knee;
And then I'll stand and stroke his silver hair,
  And be like him, and he will then love me.

William Blake

14

The sun descending in the west,
  The evening star does shine;
The birds are silent in their nest,
  And I must seek for mine.
    The moon, like a flower,
    In heaven's high bower,
    With silent delight
    Sits and smiles on the night.

Farewell, green fields and happy groves,
  Where flocks have took delight.
Where lambs have nibbled, silent moves
  The feet of angels bright;
    Unseen they pour blessing,
    And joy without ceasing,
    On each bud and blossom,
    And each sleeping bosom.

They look in every thoughtless nest,
  Where birds are cover'd warm;
They visit caves of every beast,
  To keep them all from harm.
    If they see any weeping
    That should have been sleeping,
    They pour sleep on their head,
    And sit down by their bed.

When wolves and tigers howl for prey,
  They pitying stand and weep;
Seeking to drive their thirst away,
  And keep them from the sheep.
    But if they rush dreadful,
    The angels, most heedful,
    Receive each mild spirit,
    New worlds to inherit.

And there the lion's ruddy eyes
  Shall flow with tears of gold,
And pitying the tender cries,
  And walking round the fold,
    Saying 'Wrath by His meekness,
    And by His health, sickness
    Is driven away
    From our immortal day.

'And now beside thee, bleating lamb,
  I can lie down and sleep;
Or think on Him who bore thy name,
  Graze after thee and weep.

'For, wash'd in life's river,
My bright mane for ever
Shall shine like the gold
As I guard o'er the fold.'

William Blake

15

Sir Walter Scott born, August 15, 1771.

Breathes there the man, with soul so dead,
Who never to himself hath said,
    This is my own, my native land!
Whose heart hath ne'er within him burn'd,
As home his footsteps he hath turn'd,
    From wandering on a foreign strand!
If such there breathe, go, mark him well;
For him no Minstrel raptures swell;
High though his titles, proud his name,
Boundless his wealth as wish can claim;
Despite these titles, power, and pelf,
The wretch, concentered all in self,
Living, shall forfeit fair renown,
And, doubly dying, shall go down
To the vile dust, from whence he sprung,
Unwept, unhonour'd and unsung.

O Caledonia! stern and wild,
Meet nurse for a poetic child!
Land of brown heath and shaggy wood,

Land of the mountain and the flood,
Land of my sires! what mortal hand
Can e'er untie the filial band,
That knits me to thy rugged strand?

Scott

16

To my true king I offered free from stain
Courage and faith; vain faith, and courage vain.
For him, I threw lands, honours, wealth, away,
And one dear hope, that was more prized than they.
For him I languished in a foreign clime,
Gray-haired with sorrow in my manhood's prime;
Heard on Lavernia Scargill's whispering trees,
And pined by Arno for my lovelier Tees;
Beheld each night my home in fevered sleep,
Each morning started from the dream to weep;
Till God, who saw me tried too sorely, gave
The resting-place I asked, an early grave.
Oh thou, whom chance leads to this nameless stone,
From that proud country which was once mine own,
By those white cliffs I never more must see,
By that dear language which I spake like thee,
Forget all feuds, and shed one English tear
O'er English dust. A broken heart lies here.

Lord Macaulay

17

On Como's lake the evening star
　Is trembling as before;
An azure flood, a golden bar,
There as they were before they are,
But she that loved them—she is far,
　Far from her native shore.

　　·　　·　　·　　·　　·

But could she have reveal'd to him
　Who question'd thus, the vision bright
That ere his words were said grew dim
　And vanish'd from her sight,
Easy the answer were to know
　And plain to understand,—
　　That mind and memory both must fail,
　　And life itself must slacken sail,
And thought its functions must forego,
And fancy lose its latest glow,
　Or ere that land
Could pictured be less bright and fair
To her whose home and heart are there!
That land the loveliest that eye can see
The stranger ne'er forgets, then how should she!
Henry Taylor

18

O the gleesome saunter over fields and hill-sides!
The leaves and flowers of the commonest weeds, the
    moist fresh stillness of the woods,
The exquisite smell of the earth at daybreak, and all
    through the forenoon....

O to go back to the place where I was born,
To hear the birds sing once more,
To ramble about the house and barn and over the fields
    once more,
And through the orchard and along the old lanes once
    more.

                  Walt Whitman

19

Here sparrows build upon the trees,
    And stockdove hides her nest;
The leaves are winnowed by the breeze
    Into a calmer rest;
The black-cap's song was very sweet,
    That used the rose to kiss;
It made the Paradise complete:
    My early home was this.

The red-breast from the sweetbriar bush
    Dropt down to pick the worm;
On the horse-chestnut sang the thrush,
    O'er the house where I was born;

August

The moonlight, like a shower of pearls,
    Fell o'er this 'bower of bliss,'
And on the bench sat boys and girls:
    My early home was this.

The old house stooped just like a cave,
    Thatched o'er with mosses green;
Winter around the walls would rave,
    But all was calm within;
The trees are here all green agen,
    Here bees and flowers still kiss,
But flowers and trees seemed sweeter then:
    My early home was this.

John Clare

20

Mine be a cot beside the hill;
A bee-hive's hum shall soothe my ear;
A willowy brook that turns a mill
With many a fall shall linger near.

The swallow, oft, beneath my thatch,
Shall twitter from her clay-built nest;
Oft shall the pilgrim lift the latch,
And share my meal, a welcome guest.

Around my ivy'd porch shall spring
Each fragrant flower that drinks the dew;
And Lucy, at her wheel, shall sing
In russet-gown and apron blue.

The village-church, among the trees,
Where first our marriage-vows were given,
With merry peals shall swell the breeze,
And point with taper spire to heaven.

Samuel Rogers

21

Behold her, single in the field,
Yon solitary Highland Lass!
Reaping and singing by herself;
Stop here, or gently pass!
Alone she cuts and binds the grain,
And sings a melancholy strain;
O listen! for the Vale profound
Is overflowing with the sound.

No Nightingale did ever chaunt
More welcome notes to weary bands
Of travellers in some shady haunt,
Among Arabian sands:
A voice so thrilling ne'er was heard
In spring-time from the Cuckoo-bird,
Breaking the silence of the seas
Among the farthest Hebrides.

Will no one tell me what she sings?—
Perhaps the plaintive numbers flow
For old, unhappy, far-off things,
And battles long ago:

Or is it some more humble lay,
Familiar matter of to-day?
Some natural sorrow, loss, or pain,
That has been and may be again?

Whate'er the theme, the Maiden sang
As if her song could have no ending;
I saw her singing at her work,
And o'er the sickle bending;—
I listened, motionless and still;
And, as I mounted up the hill,
The music in my heart I bore,
Long after it was heard no more.

Wordsworth

22

She stood breast high amid the corn,
Clasp'd by the golden light of morn,
Like the sweetheart of the sun,
Who many a glowing kiss had won.

On her cheek an autumn flush,
Deeply ripened;—such a blush
In the midst of brown was born,
Like red poppies grown with corn.

Round her eyes her tresses fell,
Which were blackest none could tell,
But long lashes veil'd a light,
That had else been all too bright.

And her hat, with shady brim,
Made her tressy forehead dim;—
Thus she stood amid the stooks,
Praising God with sweetest looks:—

Sure, I said, heav'n did not mean,
Where I reap thou shouldst but glean,
Lay thy sheaf adown and come,
Share my harvest and my home.

Thomas Hood

23

Not wholly in the busy world, nor quite
Beyond it, blooms the garden that I love.
News from the humming city comes to it
In sound of funeral or of marriage bells;
And, sitting muffled in dark leaves, you hear
The windy clanging of the minster clock;
Although between it and the garden lies
A league of grass, wash'd by a slow broad stream,
That, stirr'd with languid pulses of the oar,
Waves all its lazy lilies, and creeps on,
Barge-laden, to three arches of a bridge
Crown'd with the minster-towers.
                    The fields between
Are dewy-fresh, browsed by deep-udder'd kine,
And all about the large lime feathers low,
The lime a summer home of murmurous wings.

Tennyson

24

In my garden three ways meet,
　　Thrice the spot is blest;
Hermit thrush comes there to build,
　　Carrier dove to nest.

There broad-armed oaks, the copses' maze,
　　The cold sea-wind detain;
Here sultry Summer over-stays
　　When Autumn chills the plain.

Self-sown my stately garden grows;
　　The winds and wind-blown seed,
Cold April rain and colder snows
　　My hedges plant and feed.

From mountains far and valleys near
　　The harvests sown to-day
Thrive in all weathers without fear,—
　　Wild planters, plant away!

In cities high the careful crowds
　　Of woe-worn mortals darkling go,
But in these sunny solitudes
　　My quiet roses blow.

R. W. Emerson

25

And whan I was therin, y-wis,
Myn herte was ful glad of this.
For wel wende I ful sikerly
Have been in paradys erthelly;
So fair it was, that, trusteth wel,
It semed a place espirituel.
For certes, as at my devys,
Ther is no place in paradys
So good in for to dwelle or be
As in that GARDIN, thoughte me.

Chaucer

26

Here, in this sequestered close
Bloom the hyacinth and rose;
Here beside the modest stock
Flaunts the flaring hollyhock;
Here, without a pang, one sees
Ranks, conditions, and degrees.

All the seasons run their race
In this quiet resting-place;
Peach, and apricot, and fig
Here will ripen, and grow big;
Here is store and overplus,—
More had not Alcinous!

Here, in alleys cool and green,
Far ahead the thrush is seen;
Here along the southern wall
Keeps the bee his festival;
All is quiet else—afar
Sounds of toil and turmoil are.

Here be shadows large and long;
Here be spaces meet for song;
Grant, O garden-god, that I,
Now that none profane is nigh,—
Now that mood and moment please,
Find the fair Pierides!

Austin Dobson

27

What wond'rous Life is this I lead!
Ripe Apples drop about my Head.
The luscious Clusters of the Vine
Upon my Mouth do crush their Wine.
The Nectarine, and curious Peach,
Into my Hands themselves do reach.
Stumbling on Melons, as I pass,
Insnar'd with Flow'rs, I fall on Grass.

Mean while the Mind, from Pleasure less,
Withdraws into its Happyness:
The Mind, that Ocean where each Kind
Does straight its own Resemblance find;

Yet it creates, transcending these,
Far other Worlds, and other Seas;
Annihilating all that's made
To a green Thought in a green Shade.

Here at the Fountain's sliding Foot,
Or at some Fruit Tree's mossy Root,
Casting the Body's Veil aside,
My Soul into the Boughs does glide:
There, like a Bird, it sits and sings,
Then whets, and claps its silver Wings;
And, till prepar'd for longer Flight,
Waves in its Plumes the various Light.

Andrew Marvell

28

The wanton Troopers riding by,
Have shot my Fawn, and it will dye.
Ungentle-men! They cannot thrive
Who kill'd thee. Thou ne'er didst alive
Them any Harm: alas! nor cou'd
Thy Death yet do them any Good...
With sweetest Milk, and Sugar, first
I it at mine own Fingers nurs'd;
And as it grew, so every Day
It wax'd more white and sweet than they.
It had so sweet a Breath! And oft

I blush'd to see its Foot more soft,
And white, shall I say than *my* Hand?
Nay, any Lady's of the Land.
   It is a wond'rous Thing, how fleet
'Twas on those little Silver Feet.
With what a pretty skipping Grace,
It oft would challenge me the Race;
And when 'thad left me far away,
'Twould stay, and run again, and stay.
For it was nimbler much than Hinds;
And trod, as if on the Four Winds.
   I have a Garden of my own,
But so with Roses over-grown,
And Lillys, that you would it guess
To be a little Wilderness,
And all the Spring Time of the Year
It only lovèd to be there.
Among the Beds of Lillys I
Have sought it oft, where it should lye;
Yet could not, till it self would rise,
Find it, although before mine Eyes:
For, in the flaxen Lilly's Shade,
It like a Bank of Lillys laid.
Upon the Roses it would feed,
Until its Lips ev'n seem'd to bleed;
And then to me 'twould boldly trip,
And print those Roses on my Lip.
But all its chief Delight was still
On Roses thus its-self to fill;

And its pure Virgin Limbs to fold
In whitest sheets of Lillys cold.
Had it liv'd long, it would have been
Lillys without, Roses within.

Andrew Marvell

29

Ever charming, ever new,
When will the landscape tire the view!
The fountain's fall, the river's flow,
The woody valleys, warm and low;
The windy summit, wild and high,
Roughly rushing on the sky!
The pleasant seat, the ruin'd tow'r,
The naked rock, the shady bow'r:
The town and village, dome and farm,
Each give each a double charm,
As pearls upon an Ethiop's arm.

John Dyer

30

The World is too much with us; late and soon,
Getting and spending, we lay waste our powers;
Little we see in Nature that is ours;
We have given our hearts away, a sordid boon!
The Sea that bares her bosom to the moon,
The winds that will be howling at all hours

And are up-gather'd now like sleeping flowers,
For this, for everything, we are out of tune;
It moves us not.—Great God! I'd rather be
A Pagan suckled in a creed outworn,—
So might I, standing on this pleasant lea,
Have glimpses that would make me less forlorn;
Have sight of Proteus rising from the sea;
Or hear old Triton blow his wreathèd horn.

Wordsworth

3 1

Through the sheltering sycamores
Blows the wild wind from the shores,
Whilst the nations of the wheat
Bow and sway before his feet.
Where the far fields fade, and die
In the shining of the sky,
Right across the spacious plain
He is gone, and back again.
He will ruffle, as they browse,
Those old meadow-gods, the cows;
He will toss, like prancing steeds,
All the beanfields and the reeds,
Whilst the scattered clouds on high
Speed like galleons through the sky.

We alone are safe indoors,
Sheltered by the sycamores.

Frances Cornford

SEPTEMBER

Next him, *September* marched eeke on foote;
  Yet was he heavy laden with the spoyle
  Of harvests riches, which he made his boot,
  And him enricht with bounty of the soyle:
  In his one hand, as fit for harvests toyle,
  He held a knife-hook; and in th' other hand
  A paire of waights, with which he did assoyle
  Both more and lesse, where it in doubt did stand,
And equall gave to each as Justice duly scann'd.

Spenser

I

DEAR, beauteous death! the Jewel of the Just,
  Shining no where, but in the dark;
What mysteries do lie beyond thy dust;
  Could man outlook that mark!

He that hath found some fledg'd birds nest, may know
  At first sight, if the bird be flown;
But what fair Well or Grove he sings in now,
  That is to him unknown.

And yet, as Angels in some brighter dreams
  Call to the soul, when man doth sleep:
So some strange thoughts transcend our wonted theams,
  And into glory peep.

If a star were confin'd into a Tomb
  Her captive flames must needs burn there;
But when the hand that lockt her up, gives room,
  She 'l shine through all the sphære.

O Father of eternal life, and all
  Created glories under thee!
Resume thy spirit from this world of thrall
  Into true liberty.

Either disperse these mists which blot and fill,
  My perspective (still) as they pass,
Or else remove me hence unto that hill,
  Where I shall need no glass.

                                        Henry Vaughan

2

O stream descending to the sea,
  Thy mossy banks between,
The flow'rets blow, the grasses grow,
  The leafy trees are green.

In garden plots the children play,
  The fields the labourers till,
And houses stand on either hand,
  And thou descendest still.

O life descending into death,
  Our waking eyes behold,
Parent and friend thy lapse attend,
  Companions young and old.

Strong purposes our mind possess,
  Our hearts affections fill,
We toil and earn, we seek and learn,
  And thou descendest still.

O end to which our currents tend,
  Inevitable sea,
To which we flow, what do we know,
  What shall we guess of thee?

A roar we hear upon thy shore,
  As we our course fulfil;
Scarce we divine a sun will shine
  And be above us still.

A. H. Clough

3

Death, be not proud, though some have callèd thee
Mighty and dreadful, for thou art not so;
For those, whom thou think'st thou dost overthrow,
Die not, poor Death; nor yet canst thou kill me.
From rest and sleep, which but thy picture be,
Much pleasure, then from thee much more must flow:
And soonest our best men with thee do go,
Rest of their bones, and soul's delivery.
Thou'rt slave to fate, chance, kings, and desperate men,
And dost with poison, war, and sickness dwell;
And poppy or charms can make us sleep as well,
And better than thy stroke. Why swell'st thou then?
One short sleep past, we wake eternally;
And death shall be no more; Death, thou shalt die.

John Donne

4

You promise heavens free from strife,
　　Pure truth, and perfect change of will;
But sweet, sweet is this human life,
　　So sweet, I fain would breathe it still:
Your chilly stars I can forego,
This warm kind world is all I know.

　　You say there is no substance here,
　　　　One great reality above:

Back from that void I shrink in fear,
   And child-like hide myself in love:
Show me what angels feel. Till then,
I cling, a mere weak man, to men.

You bid me lift my mean desires
   From faltering lips and fitful veins
To sexless souls, ideal quires,
   Unwearied voices, wordless strains:
My mind with fonder welcome owns
One dear dead friend's remembered tones.

Forsooth the present we must give
   To that which cannot pass away;
All beauteous things for which we live
   By laws of time and space decay.
But oh, the very reason why
I clasp them, is because they die.

W. J. Cory

5

Saints have adored the lofty soul of you.
Poets have whitened at your high renown.
We stand among the many millions who
Do hourly wait to pass your pathway down.
You, so familiar, once were strange: we tried
To live as of your presence unaware.
But now in every road on every side
We see your straight and steadfast signpost there.

September

I think it like that signpost in my land,
Hoary and tall, which pointed me to go
Upward, into the hills, on the right hand,
Where the mists swim and the winds shriek and blow,
A homeless land and friendless, but a land
I did not know and that I wished to know.

(1915)   *Charles Sorley*

6

A late lark twitters from the quiet skies;
And from the west,
Where the sun, his day's work ended,
Lingers as in content,
There falls on the old, gray city
An influence luminous and serene,
A shining peace.

The smoke ascends
In a rosy-and-golden haze. The spires
Shine, and are changed. In the valley
Shadows rise. The lark sings on. The sun,
Closing his benediction,
Sinks, and the darkening air
Thrills with a sense of the triumphing night—
Night, with her train of stars
And her great gift of sleep.

So be my passing:
My task accomplished and the long day done,
My wages taken, and in my heart
Some late lark singing,
Let me be gathered to the quiet west,
The sundown splendid and serene,
Death.

W. E. Henley

7

Hope humbly then; with trembling pinions soar;
Wait the great teacher death, and God adore.
What future bliss, he gives not thee to know,
But gives that hope to be thy blessing now.
Hope springs eternal in the human breast:
Man never *is*, but always *to be* blest:
The soul, uneasy and confin'd from home,
Rests and expatiates in a life to come.
Lo, the poor Indian! whose untutor'd mind
Sees God in clouds, or hears him in the wind;
His soul, proud science never taught to stray
Far as the solar walk, or milky way;
Yet simple nature to his hope has giv'n,
Behind the cloud-topt hill, an humbler heaven;
Some safer world in depth of woods embrac'd,
Some happier island in the wat'ry waste,

Where slaves once more their native land behold,
No fiends torment, no Christians thirst for gold.
To Be, contents his natural desire,
He asks no angel's wing, no seraph's fire;
But thinks, admitted to that equal sky,
His faithful dog shall bear him company.

Pope

8

When I have seen by Time's fell hand defac'd
The rich-proud cost of outworn buried age;
When sometime lofty towers I see down-raz'd,
And brass eternal slave to mortal rage;
When I have seen the hungry ocean gain
Advantage on the kingdom of the shore,
And the firm soil win of the watery main,
Increasing store with loss, and loss with store;
When I have seen such interchange of state,
Or state itself confounded to decay;
Ruin hath taught me thus to ruminate—
That Time will come and take my love away.
  This thought is as a death, which cannot choose
  But weep to have that which it fears to lose.

Shakespeare

9

My heart leaps up when I behold
  A rainbow in the sky:
So was it when my life began;
So is it now I am a man;
So be it when I shall grow old,
  Or let me die!
The Child is father of the Man;
And I could wish my days to be
Bound each to each by natural piety.

Wordsworth

10

Thy thoughts and feelings shall not die,
Nor leave thee, when grey hairs are nigh,
A melancholy slave;
But an old age serene and bright,
And lovely as a Lapland night,
Shall lead thee to thy grave.

Wordsworth

11

The day becomes more solemn and serene
  When noon is past: there is a harmony
  In autumn, and a lustre in its sky,
Which through the summer is not heard nor seen,
As if it could not be, as if it had not been!

Shelley

September

12

The seas are quiet when the winds give o'er:
So calm are we when passions are no more!
For then we know how vain it was to boast
Of fleeting things, so certain to be lost.
Clouds of affection from our younger eyes
Conceal that emptiness which age descries.
The soul's dark cottage, batter'd and decay'd,
Lets in new light through chinks that time has made:
Stronger by weakness, wiser men become,
As they draw near to their eternal home:
Leaving the old, both worlds at once they view,
That stand upon the threshold of the new.

Edmund Waller

13

To me, fair friend, you never can be old,
For as you were when first your eye I ey'd
Such seems your beauty still. Three winters cold
Have from the forests shook three summers' pride,
Three beauteous springs to yellow autumn turn'd
In process of the seasons have I seen,
Three April perfumes in three hot Junes burn'd,
Since first I saw you fresh, which yet are green.
Ah! yet doth beauty, like a dial-hand,
Steal from his figure, and no pace perceiv'd;

So your sweet hue, which methinks still doth stand,
Hath motion, and mine eye may be deceiv'd:
  For fear of which, hear this, thou age unbred:
  Ere you were born was beauty's summer dead.

Shakespeare

14

Thy bosom is endeared with all hearts,
Which I by lacking have supposed dead,
And there reigns love, and all love's loving parts,
And all those friends which I thought buried.
How many a holy and obsequious tear
Hath dear religious love stol'n from mine eye,
As interest of the dead, which now appear
But things remov'd, that hidden in thee lie!
Thou art the grave where buried love doth live,
Hung with the trophies of my lovers gone,
Who all their parts of me to thee did give;
That due of many now is thine alone:
  Their images I lov'd I view in thee,
  And thou (all they) hast all the all of me.

Shakespeare

15

Hie away, hie away
Over bank and over brae,
Where the copsewood is the greenest,
Where the fountains glisten sheenest,

Where the lady-fern grows strongest,
Where the morning dew lies longest,
Where the black-cock sweetest sips it,
Where the fairy latest trips it:
Hie to haunts right seldom seen,
Lovely, lonesome, cool, and green,
Over bank and over brae,
Hie away, hie away.

Scott

16

Thou comest, Autumn, heralded by the rain,
  With banners, by great gales incessant fanned,
  Brighter than brightest silks of Samarcand,
  And stately oxen harnessed to thy wain!
Thou standest, like imperial Charlemagne,
  Upon thy bridge of gold; thy royal hand
  Outstretched with benedictions o'er the land,
  Blessing the farms through all thy vast domain!
Thy shield is the red harvest moon, suspended
  So long beneath the heaven's o'erhanging eaves;
  Thy steps are by the farmer's prayers attended;
Like flames upon an altar shine the sheaves;
  And, following thee, in thy ovation splendid,
  Thine almoner, the wind, scatters the golden leaves!

H. W. Longfellow

17

The length o' days ageän do shrink
An' flowers be thin in meäd, among
The eegrass a-sheenèn bright, along
Brook upon brook, an' brink by brink.

Noo starlèns do rise in vlock on wing—
Noo goocoo in nest-green leaves do sound—
Noo swallows be now a-wheelèn round—
Dip after dip, an' swing by swing.

The wheat that did leätely rustle thick
Is now up in mows that still be new,
An' yollow bevore the sky o' blue—
Tip after tip, an' rick by rick.

While now I can walk a dusty mile
I'll teäke me a day, while days be clear,
To vind a vew friends that still be dear,
Feäce after feäce, an' smile by smile.

William Barnes

18

The ground is clear. There's nar a ear
O' stannèn corn a-left out now,
Vor win' to blow or raïn to drow;
'Tis all up seäfe in barn or mow.
Here's health to them that plough'd an' zow'd;
Here's health to them that reap'd an' mow'd,

An' them that had to pitch an' lwoad,
 Or tip the rick at Harvest Hwome.
The happy zight,—the merry night,
The men's delight,—the Harvest Hwome
An' mid noo harm o' vire or storm
 Bevall the farmer or his corn;
An' ev'ry zack o' zeed gi'e back
 A hunderd-vwold so much in barn.
 An' mid his Meäker bless his store,
 His wife an' all that she 've a-bore,
 And keep all evil out o' door,
 Vrom Harvest Hwome to Harvest Hwome.

       William Barnes

19

Sweet Country life, to such unknown,
Whose lives are others, not their own!
But serving Courts, and Cities, be
Less happy, less enjoying thee.
Thou never Plow'st the Oceans foame
To seek, and bring rough Pepper home:
Nor to the Eastern Ind dost rove
To bring from thence the scorched Clove.
Nor, with the losse of thy lov'd rest,
Bring'st home the Ingot from the West.
No, thy Ambition's Master-piece
Flies no thought higher then a fleece:

Or how to pay thy Hinds, and cleere
All scores; and so to end the yeere:
But walk'st about thine own dear bounds,
Not envying others larger grounds:
For well thou know'st, *'tis not th' extent*
Of Land makes life, but sweet content.

Robert Herrick

20

One ancient hen she took delight to feed,
The plodding pattern of the busy dame;
Which, ever and anon, impell'd by need,
Into her school, begirt with chickens, came;
Such favour did her past deportment claim:
And, if neglect had lavish'd on the ground
Fragment of bread, she would collect the same;
For well she knew, and quaintly could expound,
What sin it were to waste the smallest crumb she found

Herbs too she knew, and well of each could speak,
That in her garden sip'd the silv'ry dew;
Where no vain flow'r disclos'd a gaudy streak;
But herbs for use, and physick, not a few,
Of grey renown, within those borders grew:
The tufted basil, pun-provoking thyme,
Fresh baum, and mary-gold of chearful hue;
The lowly gill, that never dares to climb;
And more I fain would sing, disdaining, here to rhyme

Yet euphrasy may not be left unsung,
That gives dim eyes to wander leagues around;
And pungent radish, biting infant's tongue;
And plantain ribb'd, that heals the reaper's wound;
And marj'ram sweet, in shepherd's posie found;
And lavender, whose pikes of azure bloom
Shall be, ere-while, in arid bundles bound,
To lurk amidst the labours of her loom,
And crown her kerchiefs clean, with mickle rare perfume.

And here trim rosemarine, that whilom crown'd
The daintiest garden of the proudest peer;
Ere, driven from its envy'd site, it found
A sacred shelter for its branches here;
Where edg'd with gold its glitt'ring skirts appear.
Oh wassel days! O customs meet and well!
Ere this was banish'd from its lofty sphere:
Simplicity then sought this humble cell,
Nor ever would she more with thane and lordling dwell.

William Shenstone

21

Jack and Joan, they think no ill,
But loving live, and merry still;
Do their weekdays' work, and pray
Devoutly on the holy day;
Skip and trip it on the green,
And help to choose the summer queen;
Lash out, at a country feast,
Their silver penny with the best.

Well can they judge of nappy ale,
And tell at large a winter tale,
Climb up to the apple loft,
And turn the crabs till they be soft.
Tib is all the father's joy,
And little Tom the mother's boy.
All their pleasure is content;
And care, to pay their yearly rent.

Joan can call by name her cows,
And deck her windows with green boughs;
She can wreaths and tutties make,
And trim with plums a bridal cake.
Jack knows what brings gain or loss;
And his long flail can stoutly toss;
Makes the hedge, which others break,
And ever thinks what he doth speak.

Now, you courtly dames and knights,
That study only strange delights;
Though you scorn the homespun grey,
And revel in your rich array:
Though your tongues dissemble deep,
And can your heads from danger keep;
Yet, for all your pomp and train,
Securer lives the silly swain.

Thomas Campion

22

Art thou poor, yet hast thou golden slumbers?
   O sweet content!
Art thou rich, yet is thy mind perplex'd?
   O punishment!
Dost thou laugh to see how fools are vex'd
To add to golden numbers, golden numbers?
O sweet content! O sweet, O sweet content!
   Work apace, apace, apace, apace;
   Honest labour bears a lovely face;
Then hey nonny nonny—hey nonny nonny!

Canst drink the waters of the crispèd spring?
   O sweet content!
Swim'st thou in wealth, yet sink'st in thine own
   tears?
   O punishment!
Then he that patiently want's burden bears,
No burden bears, but is a king, a king!
O sweet content! O sweet, O sweet content!
   Work apace, apace, apace, apace;
   Honest labour bears a lovely face;
Then hey nonny nonny—hey nonny nonny!

Thomas Dekker

23

Near yonder copse, where once the garden smil'd,
And still where many a garden flower grows wild;
There, where a few torn shrubs the place disclose,
The village preacher's modest mansion rose.
A man he was to all the country dear,
And passing rich with forty pounds a year;
Remote from towns he ran his godly race,
Nor e'er had chang'd, nor wished to change his place;
Unpractis'd he to fawn, or seek for power,
By doctrines fashion'd to the varying hour;
Far other aims his heart had learned to prize,
More skill'd to raise the wretched than to rise.
His house was known to all the vagrant train,
He chid their wand'rings, but reliev'd their pain;
The long-remember'd beggar was his guest,
Whose beard descending swept his aged breast;
The ruin'd spendthrift, now no longer proud,
Claim'd kindred there, and had his claims allow'd;
The broken soldier, kindly bade to stay,
Sat by his fire, and talk'd the night away;
Wept o'er his wounds, or tales of sorrow done,
Shoulder'd his crutch, and show'd how fields were won.
Pleas'd with his guests, the good man learn'd to glow,
And quite forgot their vices in their woe;
Careless their merits, or their faults to scan,
His pity gave ere charity began.

Thus to relieve the wretched was his pride,
And e'en his failings lean'd to Virtue's side;
But in his duty prompt at every call,
He watch'd and wept, he pray'd and felt, for all.
And, as a bird each fond endearment tries
To tempt its new-fledg'd offspring to the skies,
He tried each art, reprov'd each dull delay,
Allur'd to brighter worlds, and led the way.

Oliver Goldsmith

24

A stretch of down and a sweep of air,
    A ring of trees on the sky's far rim,
A group of stacks on the slope reaped bare,
    A flight of swallows that swirl and skim.

A flock close-massed with its shepherd grey,
    A flock thin-drawn where the sun strikes bright,
A scudding shadow, a chasing ray,
    A far road vanishing straight and white.

A village tucked in the dip of the down,
    Cottage gardens with asters starred,
Roofs here red-tiled and there thatched brown,
    Gates where hollyhocks stand on guard.

A friendly inn where the cross-roads meet,
    Sycamore shade and a close-trimmed lawn
Wall-enclosed, and a rose still sweet
    Though the robin hints of the autumn's dawn.

M McN. Sharpley

25

Noon descends around me now:
'Tis the noon of autumn's glow,
When a soft and purple mist
Like a vaporous amethyst,
Or an air-dissolvèd star
Mingling light and fragrance, far
From the curved horizon's bound
To the point of Heaven's profound,
Fills the overflowing sky;
And the plains that silent lie
Underneath, the leaves unsodden
Where the infant Frost has trodden
With his morning-wingèd feet,
Whose bright print is gleaming yet;
And the red and golden vines,
Piercing with their trellised lines
The rough, dark-skirted wilderness;
The dun and bladed grass no less,
Pointing from this hoary tower
In the windless air; the flower
Glimmering at my feet; the line
Of the olive-sandalled Apennine
In the south dimly islanded;
And the Alps, whose snows are spread
High between the clouds and sun;
And of living things each one;

And my spirit which so long
Darkened this swift stream of song,—
Interpenetrated lie
By the glory of the sky:
Be it love, light, harmony,
Odour, or the soul of all
Which from Heaven like dew doth fall,
Or the mind which feeds this verse
Peopling the lone universe.

Shelley

26

Season of mists and mellow fruitfulness,
  Close bosom-friend of the maturing sun;
Conspiring with him how to load and bless
  With fruit the vines that round the thatch-eves run
To bend with apples the moss'd cottage-trees,
  And fill all fruit with ripeness to the core;
    To swell the gourd, and plump the hazel shells
  With a sweet kernel; to set budding more,
And still more, later flowers for the bees,
Until they think warm days will never cease,
    For Summer has o'er-brimm'd their clammy cells.

Who hath not seen thee oft amid thy store?
  Sometimes whoever seeks abroad may find
Thee sitting careless on a granary floor,
  Thy hair soft-lifted by the winnowing wind;

Or on a half-reap'd furrow sound asleep,
  Drows'd with the fume of poppies, while thy hook
    Spares the next swath and all its twinèd flowers:
And sometimes like a gleaner thou dost keep
  Steady thy laden head across a brook;
  Or by a cyder-press, with patient look,
    Thou watchest the last oozings, hours by hours.

Where are the songs of Spring? Ay, where are they?
  Think not of them, thou hast thy music too,—
While barred clouds bloom the soft-dying day,
  And touch the stubble-plains with rosy hue;
Then in a wailful choir the small gnats mourn
  Among the river sallows, borne aloft
    Or sinking as the light wind lives or dies;
And full-grown lambs loud bleat from hilly bourn;
  Hedge-crickets sing; and now with treble soft
  The red-breast whistles from a garden croft;
    And gathering swallows twitter in the skies.

                                Keats

27

The dark green Summer, with its massive hues,
Fades into Autumn's tincture manifold.
A gorgeous garniture of fire and gold
The high slope of the ferny hill indues.
The mists of morn in slumbering layers diffuse
O'er glimmering rock, smooth lake, and spiked array

Of hedge-row thorns, a unity of grey.
All things appear their tangible form to lose
In ghostly vastness. But anon the gloom
Melts, as the Sun puts off his muddy veil;
And now the birds their twittering songs resume,
All Summer silent in the leafy dale.
In Spring they piped of love on every tree,
But now they sing the song of memory.

Hartley Coleridge

28

The birds that sing on autumn eves
Among the golden-tinted leaves,
Are but the few that true remain
Of budding May's rejoicing train.

Like autumn flowers that brave the frost,
And make their show when hope is lost,
These 'mong the fruits and mellow scent
Mourn not the high-sunned summer spent.

Their notes through all the jocund spring
Were mixed in merry musicking:
They sang for love the whole day long,
But now their love is all for song.

Now each hath perfected his lay
To praise the year that hastes away:
They sit on boughs apart, and vie
In single songs and rich reply.

And oft as in the copse I hear
These anthems of the dying year,
The passions, once her peace that stole,
With flattering love my heart console.

Robert Bridges

29

While not a leaf seems faded; while the fields,
With ripening harvest prodigally fair,
In brightest sunshine bask; this nipping air,
Sent from some distant clime where Winter wields
His icy scimitar, a foretaste yields
Of bitter change, and bids the flowers beware;
And whispers to the silent birds, "Prepare
Against the threatening foe your trustiest shields."
For me, who under kindlier laws belong
To Nature's tuneful quire, this rustling dry
Through leaves yet green, and yon crystalline sky,
Announce a season potent to renew,
'Mid frost and snow, the instinctive joys of song,
And nobler cares than listless summer knew.

Wordsworth

30

The gather'd clouds, a-hangèn low,
  Do meäke the woody ridge look dim;
An' rain-vill'd streams do brisker flow,
  A-risèn higher to their brim.
In the tree, from lim' to lim',
    Leaves do drop
Vrom the top, all slowly down,
Yollor, on the gloomy groun'.

The rick's a-tipp'd an' weather-brown'd,
  An' thatch'd wi' zedge a-dried an' dead;
An' orcha'd apples, red half round,
  Have all a-happer'd down, a-shed
Underneath the trees' wide head.
    Lathers long,
Rong by rong, to clim' the tall
Trees, be hung upon the wall.

The crumpled leaves be now a-shed
  In mornèn winds a-blowèn keen;
When they were green the moss wer dead,
  Now they be dead the moss is green.
Low the evenèn zun do sheen
    By the boughs,
Where the cows do swing their tails
Over merry milkers' pails.

William Barnes

OCTOBER

THEN came *October* full of merry glee:
   For, yet his noule was totty of the must,
   Which he was treading in the wine-fats see,
   And of the joyous oyle, whose gentle gust
   Made him so frollick and so full of lust:
   Upon a dreadfull Scorpion he did ride,
   The same which by *Dianaes* doom unjust
   Slew great *Orion:* and eeke by his side
He had his ploughing share, and coulter ready tyde.

                              Spenser

October

1

THE feathers of the willow
Are half of them grown yellow
  Above the swelling stream;
And ragged are the bushes,
And rusty now the rushes,
  And wild the clouded gleam.

The thistle now is older,
His stalk begins to moulder,
  His head is white as snow;
The branches all are barer,
The linnet's song is rarer,
  The robin pipeth now.

R. W. Dixon

2

Dampness upon the wall,
And leaves that fall:
Cold, and a sighing brook
That speaks of death;
That calls unto the rose
Which in my garden grows,
And with his dying prayer
Perfumes the air.

October 275

Warmth of the burning days,
Flowers ablaze,
And sound of waters heard,
And song of bird—
I garner these apart,
Though summer loses heart,
And winter draws apace
To win the race.

H. O. Meredith

3

O hushed October morning mild
Thy leaves have ripened to the fall;
To-morrow's wind, if it be wild,
Should waste them all.
The crows above the forest call;
To-morrow they may form and go.
O hushed October morning mild,
Begin the hours of this day slow,
Make the day seem to us less brief.
Hearts not averse to being beguiled,
Beguile us in the way you know;
Release one leaf at break of day;
At noon release another leaf;
One from our trees, one far away;
Retard the sun with gentle mist;
Enchant the land with amethyst.
Slow, slow!

For the grapes' sake, if they were all,
Whose leaves already are burnt with frost,
Whose clustered fruit must else be lost—
For the grapes' sake along the wall.

Robert Frost

4

Fair summer droops, droop men and beasts therefore,
So fair a summer look for never more:
All good things vanish less than in a day,
Peace, plenty, pleasure suddenly decay.
   Go not yet away, bright soul of the sad year,
   The earth is hell when thou leav'st to appear.

What, shall those flowers, that decked thy garland erst
Upon thy grave be wastefully dispersed?
O trees, consume your sap in sorrow's source,
Streams, turn to tears your tributary course.
   Go not yet hence, bright soul of the sad year,
   The earth is hell when thou leav'st to appear.

Thomas Nashe

5

Unwatch'd, the garden bough shall sway,
   The tender blossom flutter down,
   Unloved, that beech will gather brown,
This maple burn itself away;

Unloved, the sun-flower, shining fair,
  Ray round with flames her disk of seed,
  And many a rose-carnation feed
With summer spice the humming air;

Unloved, by many a sandy bar,
  The brook shall babble down the plain,
  At noon or when the lesser wain
Is twisting round the polar star;

Uncared for, gird the windy grove,
  And flood the haunts of hern and crake;
  Or into silver arrows break
The sailing moon in creek and cove;

Till from the garden and the wild
  A fresh association blow,
  And year by year the landscape grow
Familiar to the stranger's child;

As year by year the labourer tills
  His wonted glebe, or lops the glades;
  And year by year our memory fades
From all the circle of the hills.

Tennyson

6

Alfred Tennyson died October 6, 1892.

We leave the well-beloved place
  Where first we gazed upon the sky;
  The roofs, that heard our earliest cry,
Will shelter one of stranger race.

We go, but ere we go from home,
  As down the garden-walks I move,
  Two spirits of a diverse love
Contend for loving masterdom.

One whispers, here thy boyhood sung
  Long since its matin song, and heard
  The low love-language of the bird
In native hazels tassel-hung.

The other answers, 'Yea, but here
  Thy feet have stray'd in after hours
  With thy lost friend among the bowers
And this hath made them trebly dear.'

These two have striven half the day,
  And each prefers his separate claim,
  Poor rivals in a losing game,
That will not yield each other way.

I turn to go; my feet are set
  To leave the pleasant fields and farms;
  They mix in one another's arms
To one pure image of regret.

Tennyson

7

Sir Philip Sidney died October 7, 1586.

You knew, who knew not *Astrophill?*
(That I should live to say I knew,
And have not in possession still)
Things knowne permit me to renew,
  Of him you know his merit such,
  I cannot say, you heare too much.

Within these woods of *Arcadie*
He chiefe delight and pleasure tooke,
And on the mountaine *Parthenie*,
Upon the chrystall liquid brooke,
  The Muses met him ev'ry day
  That taught him sing, to write, and say.

When he descended downe the mount,
His personage seemed most divine,
A thousand graces one might count,
Upon his lovely cheerfull eine.
  To heare him speake and sweetly smile,
  You were in Paradise the while.

A sweet attractive kinde of grace,
A full assurance given by lookes,
Continuall comfort in a face,
The lineaments of Gospell bookes,
  I trowe that countenance cannot lie,
  Whose thoughts are legible in the eie.

Was never eie, did see that face,
Was never eare, did heare that tong,
Was never minde, did minde his grace,
That ever thought the travell long;
  But eies, and eares, and ev'ry thought,
  Were with his sweete perfections caught.

Spenser

8

Give pardon, blessed soule! to my bold cryes,
If they, importune, interrupt thy songe,
Which now, with joyfull notes thou sing'st among
The angel-quiristers of th' heavenly skyes.
Give pardon eke, sweet soule! to my slow eies,
That since I saw thee now it is so long;
And yet the teares that unto thee belong,
To thee as yet they did not sacrifice;
I did not know that thou wert dead before,
I did not feele the griefe I did susteine;
The greater stroke astonisheth the more,
Astonishment takes from us sense of paine:
  I stood amaz'd when others' teares begun,
  And now begin to weepe when they have done.

Henry Constable

9

Tears, idle tears, I know not what they mean,
Tears from the depth of some divine despair
Rise in the heart, and gather to the eyes,
In looking on the happy Autumn-fields,
And thinking of the days that are no more.

Fresh as the first beam glittering on a sail,
That brings our friends up from the underworld,
Sad as the last which reddens over one
That sinks with all we love below the verge;
So sad, so fresh, the days that are no more.

Ah, sad and strange as in dark summer dawns
The earliest pipe of half-awaken'd birds
To dying ears, when unto dying eyes
The casement slowly grows a glimmering square;
So sad, so strange, the days that are no more.

Dear as remember'd kisses after death,
And sweet as those by hopeless fancy feign'd
On lips that are for others; deep as love,
Deep as first love, and wild with all regret;
O Death in Life, the days that are no more.

Tennyson

10

In the dark twilight of an autumn morn
I stood within a little country-town,
Wherefrom a long acquainted path went down
To the dear village haunts where I was born;
The low of oxen on the rainy wind,
Death and the Past, came up the well-known road,
And bathed my heart with tears, but stirred my mind
To tread once more the track so long untrod;
But I was warned, 'Regrets which are not thrust
Upon thee, seek not; for this sobbing breeze
Will but unman thee; thou art bold to trust
Thy woe-worn thoughts among these roaring trees,
And gleams of by-gone playgrounds. Is't no crime
To rush by night into the arms of Time?'

C. Tennyson Turner

11

Oft in the stilly night
   Ere slumber's chain has bound me,
Fond Memory brings the light
   Of other days around me:
      The smiles, the tears
      Of boyhood's years,
   The words of love then spoken;
      The eyes that shone,
      Now dimm'd and gone,
   The cheerful hearts now broken!

Thus, in the stilly night,
   Ere slumber's chain has bound me,
Sad Memory brings the light
   Of other days around me.

When I remember all
   The friends, so link'd together,
I've seen around me fall
   Like leaves in wintry weather,
      I feel like one
      Who treads alone
   Some banquet-hall deserted,
      Whose lights are fled,
      Whose garlands dead,
   And all but he departed!
Thus, in the stilly night,
   Ere slumber's chain has bound me,
Sad Memory brings the light
   Of other days around me.

                              Thomas Moore

12

Whence that low voice?—A whisper from the heart,
That told of days long past, when here I roved
With friends and kindred tenderly beloved;
Some who had early mandates to depart,
Yet are allowed to steal my path athwart
By Duddon's side; once more do we unite,
Once more beneath the kind Earth's tranquil light;

And smothered joys into new being start.
From her unworthy seat, the cloudy stall
Of Time, breaks forth triumphant Memory;
Her glistening tresses bound, yet light and free
As golden locks of birch, that rise and fall
On gales that breathe too gently to recall
Aught of the fading year's inclemency!

Wordsworth

13

Music, when soft voices die,
Vibrates in the memory—
Odour, when sweet violets sicken,
Live within the sense they quicken.

Rose leaves, when the rose is dead,
Are heaped for the beloved's bed;
And so thy thoughts, when thou art gone,
Love itself shall slumber on.

Shelley

14

Weep no more, nor sigh nor groan,
Sorrow calls no time that's gone:
Violets pluck'd, the sweetest rain
Makes not fresh nor grow again;
Trim thy locks, look chearfully,
Fate's hidden ends eyes cannot see.

Joys as winged dreams fly fast,
Why should sadness longer last?
Grief is but a wound to woe;
Gentlest fair, mourn, mourn no moe.

John Fletcher

15

Verse, a breeze mid blossoms straying,
Where Hope clung feeding, like a bee—
Both were mine! Life went a maying
   With Nature, Hope, and Poesy,
         When I was young!

When I was young?—Ah, woful when!
Ah! for the change 'twixt Now and Then!
This breathing House not built with hands,
This body that does me grievous wrong,
O'er aery cliffs and glittering sands,
How lightly then it flashed along:—
Like those trim skiffs, unknown of yore,
On winding lakes and rivers wide,
That ask no aid of sail or oar,
That fear no spite of wind or tide!
Nought cared this body for wind or weather
When Youth and I lived in't together.
Flowers are lovely; Love is flower-like;
Friendship is a sheltering tree;

O! the joys, that came down shower-like,
Of Friendship, Love, and Liberty,
      Ere I was old!

Ere I was old? Ah woful Ere,
Which tells me, Youth's no longer here!
O Youth! for years so many and sweet,
'Tis known, that Thou and I were one,
I'll think it but a fond conceit—
It cannot be, that Thou art gone!
Thy vesper-bell hath not yet toll'd:—
And thou wert aye a masker bold!
What strange disguise hast now put on,
To make believe, that thou art gone?
I see these locks in silvery slips,
This drooping gait, this altered size:
But Spring-tide blossoms on thy lips,
And tears take sunshine from thine eyes!
Life is but thought: so think I will
That Youth and I are housemates still.

Dew-drops are the gems of morning,
But the tears of mournful eve!
Where no hope is, life's a warning
That only serves to make us grieve,
      When we are old:

That only serves to make us grieve
With oft and tedious taking-leave,

Like some poor nigh-related guest,
That may not rudely be dismist;
Yet hath outstay'd his welcome while,
And tells the jest without the smile.

S. T. Coleridge

16

Ye Fields of *Cambridge*, our dear *Cambridge*, say,
Have ye not seen us Walking ev'ry Day?
Was there a *Tree* about which did not know
    The *Love* betwixt us Two?
Henceforth, ye gentle *Trees*, for ever fade;
    Or your sad Branches thicker join,
    And into darksome Shades combine;
Dark as the *Grave* wherein my *Friend* is laid.

Henceforth no Learned *Youths* beneath you sing,
'Till all the Tuneful *Birds* t'your Boughs they bring;
No Tuneful *Birds* play with their wonted Chear,
    And call the Learned *Youths* to hear;
No whistling *Winds* through the glad Branches fly,
    But all with sad Solemnity,
    Mute and unmoved be,
Mute as the *Grave* wherein my *Friend* does lye.
Large was his Soul; as large a soul as e'er
Submitted to inform a *Body* here.
High as the Place 'twas shortly in Heav'n to have,
    But Low, and Humble as his *Grave*.

So *High*, that all the *Virtues* there did come,
   As to the chiefest Seat
   Conspicuous and Great;
So *Low*, that for *Me* too it made a room.

Abraham Cowley

17

I ran out in the morning, when the air was clean and new,
And all the grass was glittering, and grey with autumn
   dew,
I ran out to the apple tree and pulled an apple down,
And all the bells were ringing in the old grey town.

Down in the town off the bridges and the grass
They are sweeping up the leaves to let the people pass,
Sweeping up the old leaves, golden-reds and browns,
Whilst the men go to lecture with the wind in their gowns.

Frances Cornford

18

Winter in the College Garden,
   Twigs for leaves and snow for grass,
Biting blasts that sear and harden
   Where soft zephyrs used to pass,
Hidden places, white bare spaces;—
   What a change it was!

Months have passed since I beheld it:
   Soon it may be here again,

Summer's gone: grey ghosts expelled it:
   Sad's the murmur of the rain:
"Winter, winter!"—dreary hinter:
   Hear the dull refrain.

As I sit this wet October,
   Russet leaf-clouds whirling by.
Can I but be grave and sober,
   Drooping spirit, downcast eye,
Thinking dimly, brooding grimly;—
   Winter, winter's nigh?

And the world that I'm recalling:—
   Such a world of burnished snow!
Scarce a brown leaf left for falling:
   Not a green leaf left to show
How the splendid colours blended
   Twenty weeks ago!

Up and down the long white spaces,
   Where dim leaves are whirling now,
How I gazed on phantom faces,
   How I planned—no matter how!
Here I wandered, here I pondered,
   Here I made a vow.

Cold crisp renovating weather,
   Clear and colourless and bright,
This, I think, should go together
   With a mind intent on right,
Plans revolving, deeds resolving,
   Seeking for the light.

Yes, I made a vow, and wrote it
    In my heart, nine months ago:
Framed a contract—I could quote it:
    Drew a line to walk by—so:
Have I kept it? or o'erleapt it?
    Well, I hardly know.

                              J. K. Stephen

19

There's not a nook within this solemn Pass
But were an apt confessional for One
Taught by his summer spent, his autumn gone,
That Life is but a tale of morning grass
Withered at eve. From scenes of art which chase
That thought away, turn, and with watchful eyes
Feed it 'mid Nature's old felicities,
Rocks, rivers, and smooth lakes more clear than glass
Untouched, unbreathed upon. Thrice happy guest,
If from a golden perch of aspen spray
(October's workmanship to rival May)
The pensive warbler of the ruddy breast
That moral sweeten by a heaven-taught lay,
Lulling the year, with all its cares, to rest!

                              Wordsworth

20

And is there care in heaven? and is there love
    In heavenly spirits to these creatures bace,
That may compassion of their evils move?
    There is: else much more wretched were the cace

Of men, then beasts. But O th' exceeding grace
Of highest God, that loves his creatures so,
And all his workes with mercy doth embrace,
That blessed Angels, he sends to and fro,
To serve to wicked man, to serve his wicked foe.

How oft do they, their silver bowers leave,
  To come to succour us, that succour want?
  How oft do they with golden pineons, cleave
  The flitting skyes, like flying Pursuivant,
  Against foule feends to aid us militant?
  They for us fight, they watch and dewly ward,
  And their bright Squadrons round about us plant,
  And all for love, and nothing for reward:
O why should heavenly God to men have such regard?

Spenser

21

Nobly, nobly Cape Saint Vincent to the North-West died
  away;
Sunset ran, one glorious blood-red, reeking into Cadiz Bay;
Bluish mid the burning water, full in face Trafalgar lay;
In the dimmest North-East distance, dawned Gibraltar
  grand and gray;
'Here and here did England help me: how can I help
  England?'—say,
Whoso turns as I, this evening, turn to God to praise and
  pray,
While Jove's planet rises yonder, silent over Africa.

Robert Browning

22

When I have borne in memory what has tamed
Great Nations, how ennobling thoughts depart
When men change swords for ledgers, and desert
The student's bower for gold, some fears unnamed
I had, my Country—am I to be blamed?
Now, when I think of thee, and what thou art,
Verily, in the bottom of my heart,
Of those unfilial fears I am ashamed.
For dearly must we prize thee; we who find
In thee a bulwark for the cause of men;
And I by my affection was beguiled:
What wonder if a Poet now and then,
Among the many movements of his mind,
Felt for thee as a lover or a child!

Wordsworth

23

O how comely it is, and how reviving
To the spirits of just men long oppressed,
When God into the hands of their deliverer
Puts invincible might,
To quell the mighty of the earth, the oppressor,
The brute and boisterous force of violent men,
Hardy and industrious to support
Tyrannic power, but raging to pursue
The righteous and all such as honour truth!

He all their ammunition
And feats of war defeats,
With plain heroic magnitude of mind
And celestial vigour armed;
Their armouries and magazines contemns,
Renders them useless, while
With winged expedition
Swift as the lightning glance he executes
His errand on the wicked, who surprised,
Lose their defence, distracted and amazed.

Milton

24

Time's glory is to calm contending kings,
To unmask falsehood, and bring truth to light,
To stamp the seal of time in aged things,
To wake the morn, and sentinel the night,
To wrong the wronger till he render right:
    To ruinate proud buildings with thy hours,
    And smear with dust their glittering golden towers:

To fill with worm-holes stately monuments,
To feed oblivion with decay of things,
To blot old books, and alter their contents,
To pluck the quills from ancient ravens' wings,
To dry the old oak's sap, and cherish springs:
    To spoil antiquities of hammer'd steel,
    And turn the giddy round of Fortune's wheel.

Shakespeare

25

Geoffrey Chaucer died October 25, 1400.

An old man in a lodge within a park;
　　The chamber walls depicted all around
　　With portraitures of huntsman, hawk, and hound,
　　And the hurt deer. He listeneth to the lark,
Whose song comes with the sunshine through the dark
　　Of painted glass in leaden lattice bound;
　　He listeneth and he laugheth at the sound,
　　Then writeth in a book like any clerk.
He is the poet of the dawn, who wrote
　　The Canterbury Tales, and his old age
　　Made beautiful with song; and as I read
I hear the crowing cock, I hear the note
　　Of lark and linnet, and from every page
　　Rise odours of ploughed field or flowery mead.

H. W. Longfellow

26

　　Bring from the craggy haunts of birch and pine,
　　　　Thou wild wind, bring
　　Keen forest odours from that realm of thine
　　　　Upon thy wing!

　　O wind, O mighty, melancholy wind,
　　　　Blow through me, blow!
　　Thou blowest forgotten things into my mind,
　　　　From long ago.

John Todhunter

27

O wild-reävèn west winds! as you do roar on,
   The elems do rock an' the poplars do ply,
An' weäve do dreve weäve in the dark-water'd pon',—
   Oh! where do ye rise vrom, an' where do ye die?

O wild-reävèn winds! I do wish I could vlee
   Wi' you, lik' a bird o' the clouds, up above
The ridge o' the hill an' the top o' the tree,
   To where I do long vor, an' vo'k I do love.

Or else that in under theäse rock I could hear,
   In the soft-zwellèn sounds you do leäve in your road,
Zome words you mid bring me, vrom tongues that be dear,
   Vrom friends that do love me, all scatter'd abrode.

O wild-reävèn winds! if you ever do roar
   By the house an' the elems vrom where I'm a-come,
Breathe up at the window, or call at the door,
   An' tell you've a-voun' me a-thinkèn o' hwome.

William Barnes

28

O wild West Wind, thou breath of Autumn's being,
Thou, from whose unseen presence the leaves dead
Are driven, like ghosts from an enchanter fleeing,

Yellow, and black, and pale, and hectic red,
Pestilence-stricken multitudes: O thou,
Who chariotest to their dark wintry bed

The wingèd seeds, where they lie cold and low,
Each like a corpse within its grave, until
Thine azure sister of the Spring shall blow

Her clarion o'er the dreaming earth, and fill
(Driving sweet buds like flocks to feed in air)
With living hues and odours plain and hill:

Wild Spirit, which art moving everywhere;
Destroyer and preserver; hear, oh, hear!

Shelley

29

Sir Walter Raleigh beheaded, October 29, 1618.

Give me my Scallop-shell of Quiet;
My Staff of Faith to walk upon;
My Scrip of Joy, immortall Diet;
My Bottle of Salvation;
My Gown of Glory (Hopes true gage);
And thus I'le take my *Pilgrimage.*
Bloud must be my Bodies Balmer,—
No other Balm will there be given;
Whil'st my Soul, like quiet Palmer,
Travelleth towards the Land of Heaven;
Over the silver Mountains,
Where spring the Nectar Fountains.
There will I kisse the Bowl of Blisse,
And drink mine everlasting fill,
Upon every Milken hill.
My Soul will be a-drie before,
But after, it will thirst no more.

Even such is time, that takes on trust
Our youth, our joyes, our all we have,
And pays us but with Earth and Dust;
Who, in the dark and silent Grave,
(When we have wandred all our ways,)
Shuts up the story of our days:
But from this Earth, this Grave, this Dust,
My God shall raise me up, I trust!

Sir Walter Raleigh

30

Look as the flow'r, which ling'ringly doth fade,
The morning's darling late, the summer's queen,
Spoil'd of that juice which kept it fresh and green,
As high as it did raise, bows low the head:
Just so the pleasures of my life being dead,
Or in their contraries but only seen,
With swifter speed declines than erst it spread,
And, blasted, scarce now shews what it hath been.
Therefore, as doth the pilgrim, whom the night
Hastes darkly to imprison on his way,
Think on thy home, my soul, and think aright
Of what's yet left thee of life's wasting day:
    Thy sun posts westward, passed is thy morn,
    And twice it is not given thee to be born.

William Drummond

31

That time of year thou mayst in me behold
When yellow leaves, or none, or few, do hang
Upon those boughs which shake against the cold,
Bare ruin'd choirs where late the sweet birds sang.
In me thou see'st the twilight of such day
As after sunset fadeth in the west,
Which by and by black night doth take away,
Death's second self, that seals up all in rest.
In me thou see'st the glowing of such fire
That on the ashes of his youth doth lie,
As the death-bed whereon it must expire,
Consumed with that which it was nourish'd by.
　　This thou perceiv'st, which makes thy love more
　　　　strong,
　　To love that well which thou must leave ere long.
Shakespeare

NOVEMBER

NEXT was *November*, he full grosse and fat,
    As fed with lard, and that right well might seeme;
    For he had been a fatting hogs of late,
    That yet his browes with sweat, did reek and steem,
    And yet the season was full sharp and breem;
    In planting eeke he took no small delight:
    Whereon he rode, not easie was to deeme;
    For it a dreadfull *Centaure* was in sight,
The seed of *Saturne*, and faire *Nais*, *Chiron* hight.

Spenser

I

Joy of my life! while left me here,
        And still my Love!
How in thy absence thou dost steere
        Me from above!
        A life well lead
        This truth commends,
        With quick or dead
        It never ends.

Stars are of mighty use: The night
        Is dark, and long;
The Rode foul, and where one goes right,
        Six may go wrong.
        One twinkling ray
        Shot o'er some cloud,
        May clear much way
        And guide a croud.

Gods Saints are shining lights: who stays
        Here long must passe
O're dark hills, swift streames, and steep ways
        As smooth as glasse;
        But these all night,
        Like Candles, shed
        Their beams, and light
        Us into bed.

They are (indeed) our Pillar-fires
 Seen as we go,
They are that Cities shining spires
 We travell too;
 A swordlike gleame
 Kept man for sin
 First *Out*; this beame
 Will guide him *In*.

Henry Vaughan

2

Ye have been fresh and green,
 Ye have been fill'd with flowers:
And ye the Walks have been
 Where Maids have spent their houres.

You have beheld, how they
 With *Wicker Arks* did come,
To kisse, and beare away
 The richer Couslips home.

Y'ave heard them sweetly sing,
 And seen them in a Round:
Each Virgin, like a Spring,
 With Hony-succles crown'd.

But now, we see, none here,
 Whose silv'rie feet did tread,
And with dishevell'd Haire,
 Adorn'd this smoother Mead.

November

Like Unthrifts, having spent,
  Your stock, and needy grown,
Y'are left here to lament
  Your poore estates, alone.

Robert Herrick

3

The mellow year is hastening to its close;
The little birds have almost sung their last,
Their small notes twitter in the dreary blast—
That shrill-piped harbinger of early snows;
The patient beauty of the scentless rose,
Oft with the Morn's hoar crystal quaintly glass'd,
Hangs, a pale mourner for the summer past,
And makes a little summer where it grows:
In the chill sunbeam of the faint brief day
The dusky waters shudder as they shine,
The russet leaves obstruct the straggling way
Of oozy brooks, which no deep banks define,
And the gaunt woods, in ragged, scant array,
Wrap their old limbs with sombre ivy twine.

Hartley Coleridge

4

Autumn, I love thy parting look to view
  In cold November's day, so bleak and bare,
When, thy life's dwindled thread worn nearly thro',
  With ling'ring, pott'ring pace, and head bleach'd bare,

Thou, like an old man, bidd'st the world adieu.
  I love thee well: and often, when a child,
Have roam'd the bare brown heath a flower to find;
  And in the moss-clad vale, and wood-bank wild
Have cropt the little bell-flowers, pearly blue,
  That trembling peep the shelt'ring bush behind.
When winnowing north-winds cold and bleaky blew.
  How have I joy'd, with dithering hands, to find
Each fading flower; and still how sweet the blast,
Would bleak November's hour restore the joy that's past.

John Clare

5

Not always fall of leaf nor ever spring,
No endless night yet not eternal day;
The saddest birds a season find to sing,
The roughest storm a calm may soon allay;
Thus with succeeding turns God tempereth all,
That man may hope to rise yet fear to fall.

A chance may win that by mischance was lost;
The well that holds no great, takes little fish;
In some things all, in all things none are cross'd;
Few all they need, but none have all they wish;
Unmeddled joys here to no man befall,
Who least hath some, who most hath never all.

Robert Southwel

6

What is gold worth, say,
Worth for work or play,
Worth to keep or pay,
Hide or throw away,
      Hope about or fear?
What is love worth, pray?
      Worth a tear?

Golden on the mould
Lie the dead leaves roll'd
Of the wet woods old,
Yellow leaves and cold,
      Woods without a dove;
Gold is worth but gold;
      Love's worth love.

A. C. Swinburne

7

Leaves have their time to fall,
And flowers to wither at the north wind's breath,
   And stars to set—but all,
Thou hast *all* seasons for thine own, O Death!

   Day is for mortal care,
Eve, for glad meetings round the joyous hearth,
Night, for the dreams of sleep, the voice of prayer—
But all for thee, thou mightiest of the earth.

We know when moons shall wane,
When summer birds from far shall cross the sea,
When autumn's hue shall tinge the golden grain—
But who shall teach us when to look for thee!

Leaves have their time to fall,
And flowers to wither at the north wind's breath,
And stars to set—but all—
Thou hast *all* seasons for thine own, O Death!

Felicia Hemans

8

John Milton died November 8, 1674.

When I consider how my light is spent,
Ere half my days in this dark world and wide,
And that one talent which is death to hide
Lodged with me useless, though my soul more bent
To serve therewith my Maker, and present
My true account, lest He returning chide;
'Doth God exact day-labour, light denied?'
I fondly ask: but Patience, to prevent
That murmur, soon replies, 'God doth not need
Either man's work, or his own gifts. Who best
Bear his mild yoke, they serve him best: his state
Is kingly: thousands at his bidding speed,
And post o'er land and ocean without rest;
They also serve who only stand and wait.'

Milton

Thus with the year
Seasons return; but not to me returns
Day, or the sweet approach of even or morn,
Or sight of vernal bloom, or summer's rose,
Or flocks, or herds, or human face divine;
But cloud instead and ever-during dark
Surrounds me, from the cheerful ways of men
Cut off, and, for the book of knowledge fair,
Presented with a universal blank
Of Nature's works, to me expunged and rased,
And wisdom at one entrance quite shut out.
So much the rather thou, Celestial Light,
Shine inward, and the mind through all her powers
Irradiate; there plant eyes; all mist from thence
Purge and disperse, that I may see and tell
Of things invisible to mortal sight.

Milton

9

How large that thrush looks on the bare thorn-tree!
    A swarm of such, three little months ago,
    Had hidden in the leaves and let none know
Save by the outburst of their minstrelsy.
A white flake here and there—a snow-lily
    Of last night's frost—our naked flower-beds hold;
    And for a rose-flower on the darkling mould
The hungry redbreast gleams. No bloom, no bee.

The current shudders to its ice-bound sedge:
  Nipped in their bath, the stark reeds one by one
  Flash each its clinging diamond in the sun:
'Neath winds which for this Winter's sovereign pledge
Shall curb great king-masts to the ocean's edge
  And leave memorial forest-kings o'erthrown.

D. G. Rossetti

10

There was a day, ere yet the autumn closed,
When, ere her wintry wars, the earth reposed,
When from the yellow weed the feathery crown,
Light as the curling smoke, fell slowly down;
When the wing'd insect settled in our sight,
And waited wind to recommence her flight;
When the wide river was a silver sheet,
And on the ocean slept th' unanchor'd fleet;
When from our garden, as we look'd above,
There was no cloud, and nothing seem'd to move.

George Crabbe

11

I dreamed that overhead
I saw in twilight grey
The Army of the Dead
Marching upon its way,

November

So still and passionless,
With faces so serene,
That scarcely could one guess
Such men in war had been.

No mark of hurt they bore,
Nor smoke, nor bloody stain;
Nor suffered any more
Famine, fatigue, or pain;
Nor any lust of hate
Now lingered in their eyes—
Who have fulfilled their fate,
Have lost all enmities.

A new and greater pride
So quenched the pride of race
That foes marched side by side
Who once fought face to face.
That ghostly army's plan
Knows but one race, one rod—
All nations there are Man,
And the one King is God.

No longer on their ears
The bugle's summons falls;
Beyond these tangled spheres
The Archangel's trumpet calls;
And by that trumpet led,
Far up the exalted sky,

The Army of the Dead
Goes by, and still goes by—
Look upward, standing mute;
 Salute!

Barry Pain

12

On seas where every pilot fails
 A thousand thousand ships to-day
Ride with a moaning in their sails,
 Through winds grey and waters grey.

They are the ships of grief. They go
 As fleets are derelict and driven,
Estranged from every port they know,
 Scarce asking fortitude of heaven.

No, do not hail them. Let them ride
 Lonely as they would lonely be...
There is an hour will prove the tide,
 There is a sun will strike the sea.

John Drinkwater

13

Arthur Hugh Clough died November 13, 1861.

Hear it, O Thyrsis, still our Tree is there!—
 Ah, vain! These English fields, this upland dim,
 These brambles pale with mist engarlanded,

That lone, sky-pointing tree, are not for him.
To a boon southern country he is fled,
And now in happier air,
Wandering with the great Mother's train divine
(And purer or more subtle soul than thee,
I trow, the mighty Mother doth not see!)
Within a folding of the Apennine,

Thou hearest the immortal strains of old.
Putting his sickle to the perilous grain
In the hot cornfield of the Phrygian king,
For thee the Lityerses song again
Young Daphnis with his silver voice doth sing;
Sings his Sicilian fold,
His sheep, his hapless love, his blinded eyes;
And how a call celestial round him rang
And heavenward from the fountain-brink he sprang,
And all the marvel of the golden skies.

Matthew Arnold

14

The old gilt vane and spire receive
The last beam eastward striking;
The first shy bat to peep at eve
Has found her to his liking.
The western heaven is dull and grey,
The last red glow has followed day.

The late, last rook is housed and will
With cronies lie till morrow;
If there's a rook loquacious still

In dream he hunts a furrow,
And flaps behind a spectre team,
Or ghostly scarecrows walk his dream.

Ralph Hodgson

15

Keen, fitful gusts are whispering here and there
  Among the bushes, half leafless and dry;
  The stars look very cold about the sky,
And I have many miles on foot to fare;
Yet feel I little of the cool bleak air,
  Or of the dead leaves rustling drearily,
  Or of those silver lamps that burn on high,
Or of the distance from home's pleasant lair:
For I am brimfull of the friendliness
  That in a little cottage I have found;
Of fair-hair'd Milton's eloquent distress,
  And all his love for gentle Lycid' drown'd;
Of lovely Laura in her light green dress,
  And faithful Petrarch gloriously crown'd.

Keats

16

Wings have we,—and as far as we can go
We may find pleasure; wilderness and wood,
Blank ocean and mere sky, support that mood
Which with the lofty sanctifies the low.

Dreams, books, are each a world; and books, we know,
Are a substantial world, both pure and good:
Round these, with tendrils strong as flesh and blood,
Our pastime and our happiness will grow.
There find I personal themes, a plenteous store,
Matter wherein right voluble I am,
To which I listen with a ready ear;
Two shall be named, pre-eminently dear,—
The gentle lady married to the Moor;
And heavenly Una with her milk-white Lamb.

Wordsworth

17

'Tis a dull sight
   To see the year dying,
When winter winds
   Set the yellow wood sighing:
      Sighing, Oh! sighing.

When such a time cometh,
   I do retire
Into an old room
   Beside a bright fire:
      Oh, pile a bright fire!

And there I sit
   Reading old things,
Of knights and lorn damsels,
   While the wind sings—
      Oh, drearily sings!

I never look out,
   Nor attend to the blast;
For all to be seen
   Is the leaves falling fast:
      Falling, falling!

But close at the hearth,
   Like a cricket, sit I,
Reading of summer
   And chivalry—
      Gallant chivalry!

Then with an old friend,
   I talk of our youth—
How 'twas gladsome, but often
   Foolish, forsooth:
      But gladsome, gladsome!

Or to get merry
   We sing some old rhyme
That made the wood ring again
   In summer time—
      Sweet summer time!

Then go we to smoking
   Silent and snug;
Nought passes between us
   Save a brown jug—
      Sometimes!

And sometimes a tear
　Will rise in each eye,
Seeing the two old friends
　So merrily—
　　So merrily!

And ere to bed
　Go we, go we,
Down on the ashes
　We kneel on the knee,
　　Praying together!

Thus, then, live I,
　Till, 'mid all the gloom,
By heaven! the bold sun
　Is with me in the room,
　　Shining, shining!

Then the clouds part,
　Swallows soaring between;
The spring is alive,
　And the meadows are green!

I jump up, like mad,
　Break the old pipe in twain,
And away to the meadows,
　The meadows again!

Edward FitzGerald

18

The seas of England are our old delight;
Let the loud billow of the shingly shore
Sing freedom on her breezes evermore
To all earth's ships that sailing heave in sight!

The gaunt sea-nettle be our fortitude,
Sturdily blowing where the clear wave sips;
O, be the glory of our men and ships
Rapturous, woe-unheeding hardihood!

There is great courage in a land that hath
Liberty guarded by the unearthly seas;
And ev'n to find peace at the last in these
How many a sailor hath sailed down to death!

Their names are like a splendour in old song;
Their record shines like bays along the years;
Their jubilation is the cry man hears
Sailing sun-fronted the vast deeps among.

The seas of England are our old delight;
Let the loud billow of the shingly shore
Sing freedom on her breezes evermore
To all earth's ships that sailing heave in sight!

Walter de la Mare

19

This song the sea sings strikes the inner ear
    O'erlaid and deafened by the city's din,
    The odours of the sea and down let in
Lost thoughts of many an ancient hope and fear:
The wind blows through me, carrying clean away
    The dust that long has settled on my heart—
    The flying motes blown in from street and mart
And all the idle business of the day—
The second self—all men's by fate or choice—
    Drops from me like a garment: I am one
    With those wild sons of Earth whose race was run,
        Long ages ere she brought forth one like me,
And so she hails me, with a mother's voice,
    A primal man beside a primal sea.

Walter Hogg

20

It keeps eternal whisperings around
    Desolate shores, and with its mighty swell
    Gluts twice ten thousand caverns, till the spell
Of Hecate leaves them their old shadowy sound.
Often 'tis in such gentle temper found,
    That scarcely will the very smallest shell
    Be moved for days from whence it sometime fell,
When last the winds of heaven were unbound.

Oh ye! who have your eye-balls vexed and tired,
  Feast them upon the wideness of the Sea;
Oh ye! whose ears are dinn'd with uproar rude,
  Or fed too much with cloying melody,—
Sit ye near some old cavern's mouth, and brood
Until ye start, as if the sea-nymphs quired!

Keats

21

Where lies the Land to which yon Ship must go?
Fresh as a lark mounting at break of day,
Festively she puts forth in trim array;
Is she for tropic suns, or polar snow?
What boots the enquiry?—Neither friend nor foe
She cares for; let her travel where she may,
She finds familiar names, a beaten way
Ever before her, and a wind to blow.
Yet still I ask, what haven is her mark?
And, almost as it was when ships were rare,
(From time to time, like Pilgrims, here and there
Crossing the waters) doubt, and something dark,
Of the old Sea some reverential fear,
Is with me at thy farewell, joyous Bark!

Wordsworth

22

Break, break, break,
  On thy cold gray stones, O Sea!
And I would that my tongue could utter
  The thoughts that arise in me.

O well for the fisherman's boy,
  That he shouts with his sister at play!
O well for the sailor lad,
  That he sings in his boat on the bay!

And the stately ships go on
  To their haven under the hill;
But O for the touch of a vanish'd hand,
  And the sound of a voice that is still!

Break, break, break,
  At the foot of thy crags, O Sea!
But the tender grace of a day that is dead
  Will never come back to me.

Tennyson

23

Cold grew the foggy morn, the day was brief,
Loose on the cherry hung the crimson leaf;
The dew dwelt ever on the herb; the woods
Roar'd with strong blasts, with mighty showers the
    floods:
All green was vanish'd, save of pine and yew,
That still display'd their melancholy hue;
Save the green holly with its berries red,
And the green moss that o'er the gravel spread.

George Crabbe

24

A spirit haunts the year's last hours
Dwelling amid these yellowing bowers:
    To himself he talks;
For at eventide, listening earnestly,
At his work you may hear him sob and sigh
    In the walks;
    Earthward he boweth the heavy stalks
Of the mouldering flowers:
  Heavily hangs the broad sunflower
    Over its grave i' the earth so chilly;
  Heavily hangs the hollyhock,
    Heavily hangs the tiger-lily.

The air is damp, and hush'd, and close,
As a sick man's room when he taketh repose
    An hour before death;
My very heart faints and my whole soul grieves
At the moist rich smell of the rotting leaves,
    And the breath
    Of the fading edges of box beneath,
And the year's last rose.
  Heavily hangs the broad sunflower
    Over its grave i' the earth so chilly;
  Heavily hangs the hollyhock,
    Heavily hangs the tiger-lily.

Tennyson

25

Now gaze the stags upon the glassy brooks,
  Then slowly through their leafy walks retire,
The huntsman from his close-shut casement looks,
  And heaps new wood upon his blazing fire;
The lowing kine, from out the flow'ry meads,
  Now pale and frozen, under shelter stand,
The ox within his stall contented feeds,
  And plough and wain are idle on the land;
The hind within the house his labour plies,
  The dreaming hound upon the hearth is laid,
The flapping sea-gull from the coastward flies,
  And robin now can perch on axe and spade:
This, this is Autumn, when the freezing sky,
And mournful air proclaim the Winter nigh.

Lord Thurlow

26

William Cowper born, November 26, 1731.

Where once we dwelt our name is heard no more,
Children not thine have trod my nurs'ry floor;
And where the gard'ner Robin, day by day,
Drew me to school along the public way,
Delighted with my bauble coach, and wrapt
In scarlet mantle warm, and velvet capt,
'Tis now become a history little known,
That once we call'd the past'ral house our own.

Short-liv'd possession! but the record fair
That mem'ry keeps of all thy kindness there,
Still outlives many a storm that has effac'd
A thousand other themes less deeply trac'd.
Thy nightly visits to my chamber made,
That thou might'st know me safe and warmly laid;
Thy morning bounties ere I left my home,
The biscuit, or confectionary plum;
The fragrant waters on my cheek bestow'd
By thy own hand, till fresh they shone and glow'd;
All this, and more endearing still than all,
Thy constant flow of love, that knew no fall,
Ne'er roughen'd by those cataracts and brakes
That humour interpos'd too often makes;
All this still legible in mem'ry's page,
And still to be so, to my latest age,
Adds joy to duty, makes me glad to pay
Such honours to thee as my numbers may;
Perhaps a frail memorial, but sincere,
Not scorn'd in heav'n, though little notic'd here.

William Cowper

27

Now winter nights enlarge
The number of their houres;
And clouds their stormes discharge
Upon the ayrie towres.
Let now the chimneys blaze
And cups o'erflow with wine,

Let well-tun'd words amaze
    With harmonie divine.
Now yellow waxen lights
    Shall waite on hunny Love,
While youthfull Revels, Masks, and Courtly sights,
    Sleepes leaden spels remove.

This time doth well dispence
    With lovers' long discourse;
Much speech hath some defence,
    Though beauty no remorse.
All doe not all things well;
    Some measures comely tread;
    Some knotted Ridles tell;
        Some Poems smoothly read.
    The Summer hath his joyes,
        And Winter his delights;
    Though Luve and all his pleasures are but toyes,
    They shorten tedious nights.

                              Thomas Campion

28

Oh Winter, ruler of th' inverted year,
Thy scatter'd hair with sleet like ashes fill'd,
Thy breath congeal'd upon thy lips, thy cheeks
Fring'd with a beard made white with other snows
Than those of age, thy forehead wrapt in clouds,
A leafless branch thy sceptre, and thy throne
A sliding car, indebted to no wheels,
But urg'd by storms along its slipp'ry way,

I love thee, all unlovely as thou seem'st,
And dreaded as thou art! Thou hold'st the sun
A pris'ner in the yet undawning east,
Short'ning his journey between morn and noon,
And hurrying him, impatient of his stay,
Down to the rosy west; but kindly still
Compensating his loss with added hours
Of social converse and instructive ease,
And gath'ring, at short notice, in one group
The family dispers'd, and fixing thought,
Not less dispers'd by day-light and its cares.
I crown thee king of intimate delights,
Fire-side enjoyments, home-born happiness,
And all the comforts that the lowly roof
Of undisturb'd retirement, and the hours
Of long uninterrupted ev'ning, know.

William Cowper

29

It was frosty winter season,
And fair Flora's wealth was geason[1].
Meads that erst with green were spread,
With choice flowers diap'red,
Had tawny veils; cold had scanted
What the spring and nature planted.
Leafless boughs there might you see,
All except fair Daphne's tree:
On their twigs no birds perched;
Warmer coverts now they searched;

[1] Withered.

And by nature's secret reason,
Framed their voices to the season,
With their feeble tunes bewraying,
How they grieved the spring's decaying.
Frosty winter thus had gloomed
Each fair thing that summer bloomed;
Fields were bare, and trees unclad,
Flowers withered, birds were sad.

Robert Greene

30

I'm glad we have wood in store awhile,
Avore all the ground 's a-vroze awhile;
Vor soon we must shut the door awhile
Vrom wind that's a-whirlèn snow.

The zwallows have all a-hied away,
The flowers have now a-died away,
An' boughs, wi' their leaves a-dried away,
In wind do goo to and fro.

Noo rwose is a-bloomèn red to-day,
Noo pink vor your breast or head to-day,
A-deckèn the geärden bed to-day,
Do linger a-noddèn low.

Zoo now gi'e your cheäks a bloom to-night,
Where vier do het the room to-night,
A-drevèn away the gloom to-night,
While winterly wind do blow.

William Barnes

DECEMBER

And after him, came next the chill *December*:
  Yet he through merry feasting which he made,
  And great bonfires, did not the cold remember;
  His Saviour's birth his mind so much did glad:
  Upon a shaggy-bearded Goat he rode,
  The same wherewith *Dan Jove* in tender years,
  They say, was nourisht by th' *Idaean* mayd;
  And in his hand a broad deepe boawle he beares;
Of which, he freely drinks an health to all his peeres.

Spenser

I

In a drear-nighted December,
Too happy, happy tree,
Thy branches ne'er remember
Their green felicity:
The north cannot undo them,
With a sleety whistle through them;
Nor frozen thawings glue them
From budding at the prime.

In a drear-nighted December,
Too happy, happy brook,
Thy bubblings ne'er remember
Apollo's summer look;
But with a sweet forgetting,
They stay their chrystal fretting,
Never, never petting
About the frozen time.

Ah! would 'twere so with many
A gentle girl and boy!
But were there ever any
Writh'd not at passed joy?
To know the change and feel it,
When there is none to heal it,
Nor numbed sense to steel it,
Was never said in rhyme.

Keats

2

Whilome in youth, when flowrd my joyfull spring,
Like Swallow swift I wandred here and there;
For heate of heedlesse lust me so did sting,
That I of doubted daunger had no feare:
  I went the wastefull woodes and forest wide,
  Withouten dreade of Wolves to bene espyed.

I wont to raunge amydde the mazie thickette,
And gather nuttes to make me Christmas game,
And joyed oft to trace the trembling Pricket,
Or hunt the hartlesse hare til shee were tame.
  What recked I of wintrye ages waste?—
  Tho deemed I my spring would ever laste.

How often have I scaled the craggie Oke,
All to dislodge the Raven of her nest?
How have I wearied with many a stroke
The stately Walnut-tree, the while the rest
  Under the tree fell all for nuts at strife?
  For ylike to me was libertee and lyfe.

Spenser

3

  Weighing the stedfastness and state
Of some mean things which here below reside,
Where birds like watchful Clocks the noiseless date
  And Intercourse of times divide,

December

Where Bees at night get home and hive, and flowrs
    Early, aswel as late,
Rise with the Sun, and set in the same bowrs;
    I would (said I) my God would give
The staidness of these things to man! for these
To his divine appointments ever cleave,
    And no new business breaks their peace;
The birds nor sow, nor reap, yet sup and dine,
    The flowres without clothes live,
Yet *Solomon* was never drest so fine.

    Man hath stil either toyes, or Care,
He hath no root, nor to one place is ty'd,
But ever restless and Irregular
    About this Earth doth run and ride,
He knows he hath a home, but scarce knows where,
    He sayes it is so far
That he hath quite forgot how to go there.

    He knocks at all doors, strays and roams,
Nay hath not so much wit as some stones have
Which in the darkest nights point to their homes,
    By some hid sense their Maker gave;
Man is the shuttle to whose winding quest
    And passage through these looms
God order'd motion, but ordain'd no rest.

Henry Vaughan

4

Say not, the struggle nought availeth,
The labour and the wounds are vain,
The enemy faints not, nor faileth,
And as things have been they remain.

If hopes were dupes, fears may be liars;
It may be, in yon smoke concealed,
Your comrades chase e'en now the fliers,
And, but for you, possess the field.

For while the tired waves, vainly breaking,
Seem here no painful inch to gain,
Far back, through creeks and inlets making,
Comes silent, flooding in, the main.

And not by eastern windows only,
When daylight comes, comes in the light;
In front the sun climbs slow, how slowly,
But westward, look, the land is bright.

A. H. Clough

5

Alas! what boots it with incessant care
To tend the homely, slighted, shepherd's trade,
And strictly meditate the thankless Muse?
Were it not better done, as others use,
To sport with Amaryllis in the shade,
Or with the tangles of Neæra's hair?

Fame is the spur that the clear spirit doth raise
(That last infirmity of noble mind)
To scorn delights, and live laborious days;
But the fair guerdon when we hope to find,
And think to burst out into sudden blaze,
Comes the blind Fury with the abhorred shears,
And slits the thin-spun life. 'But not the praise,'
Phoebus replied, and touched my trembling ears:
'Fame is no plant that grows on mortal soil,
Nor in the glistering foil
Set off to the world, nor in broad rumour lies,
But lives, and spreads aloft by those pure eyes,
And perfect witness of all-judging Jove;
As he pronounces lastly on each deed,
Of so much fame in heaven expect thy meed.'

Milton

6

Good Muse, rock me asleep
    With some sweet harmony;
This weary eye is not to keep
    Thy wary company.

Sweet Love, begone awhile;
    Thou know'st my heaviness;
Beauty is born but to beguile
    My heart of happiness.

See how my little flock,
    That loved to feed on high,
Do headlong tumble down the rock
    And in the valley die.

The bushes and the trees
    That were so fresh and green,
Do all their dainty colour leese,
    And not a leaf is seen.

The blackbird and the thrush
    That made the woods to ring,
With all the rest, are now at hush
    And not a note they sing.

Sweet Philomel, the bird
    That hath the heavenly throat,
Doth now, alas! not once afford
    Recording of a note.

The flowers have had a frost,
    Each herb hath lost her savour,
And Phyllida the fair hath lost
    The comfort of her favour.

Now all these careful sights
    So kill me in conceit,
That how to hope upon delights,
    It is but mere deceit.

And therefore, my sweet Muse,
    Thou know'st what help is best;
Do now thy heavenly cunning use
    To set my heart at rest:

And in a dream bewray
    What fate shall be my friend,
Whether my life shall still decay,
    Or when my sorrow end.

Nicholas Breton

7

When Chance or cruel Business parts us Two,
    What do our *Souls* I wonder do?
    Whilst Sleep does our dull Bodies tie,
Methinks at home they should not stay,
Content with *Dreams*, but boldly fly
Abroad, and meet each other half the way.

Sure they do meet, enjoy each other there,
    And mix I know not *How*, or *Where*.
    Their Friendly Lights together twine,
Though we perceiv't not to be so,
Like loving *Stars* which oft combine,
Yet not themselves their own *Conjunctions* know.

'Twere an ill World, I'll swear, for ev'ry Friend,
    If *Distance* could their *Union* end:

But *Love* it self does far advance
Above the Pow'r of *Time* and *Space*,
It scorns such outward *Circumstance*,
His *Time's for ever, ev'ry where his Place*.

Abraham Cowley

8

Come, Sleep: O Sleep! the certain knot of peace,
The baiting place of wit, the balm of woe,
  The poor man's wealth, the prisoner's release,
Th' indifferent judge between the high and low;
  With shield of proof shield me from out the press
Of those fierce darts, despair at me doth throw:
  O make in me those civil wars to cease;
I will good tribute pay, if thou do so.
  Take thou of me, smooth pillows, sweetest bed;
A chamber deaf to noise, and blind to light;
  A rosy garland, and a weary head:
And if these things, as being thine by right,
  Move not thy heavy grace, thou shalt, in me,
  Livelier than elsewhere, *Stella's* image see.

Sir Philip Sidney

9

Betwixt mine eye and heart a league is took,
And each doth good turns now unto the other:
When that mine eye is famish'd for a look,
Or heart in love with sighs himself doth smother,

With my love's picture then my eye doth feast,
And to the painted banquet bids my heart;
Another time mine eye is my heart's guest,
And in his thoughts of love doth share a part:
So, either by thy picture or my love,
Thyself away art present still with me;
For thou not farther than my thoughts canst move,
And I am still with them and they with thee;
 Or, if they sleep, thy picture in my sight
 Awakes my heart to heart's and eye's delight.

Shakespeare

10

So, my proud soul, so you, whose shining force
 Had galloped with me to eternity,
Stand now, appealing like a tired horse:
 Unharness me.

O passionate world; O faces of my friends!
 O half-grasped meanings, intricate and deep!
Sudden, as with a child, the tumult ends,
 Silenced by sleep.

Frances Cornford

11

From low to high doth dissolution climb,
And sink from high to low, along a scale
Of awful notes, whose concord shall not fail;
A musical but melancholy chime,

Which they can hear who meddle not with crime,
Nor avarice, nor over-anxious care.
Truth fails not; but her outward forms that bear
The longest date do melt like frosty rime,
That in the morning whitened hill and plain
And is no more; drop like the tower sublime
Of yesterday, which royally did wear
His crown of weeds, but could not even sustain
Some casual shout that broke the silent air,
Or the unimaginable touch of Time.

Wordsworth

12

Robert Browning died December 12, 1889.

There is delight in singing, tho' none hear
Beside the singer: and there is delight
In praising, tho' the praiser sit alone
And see the praised far off him, far above.
Shakespeare is not our poet, but the world's,
Therefore on him no speech! and brief for thee,
Browning! Since Chaucer was alive and hale,
No man hath walked along our roads with step
So active, so inquiring eye, or tongue
So varied in discourse. But warmer climes
Give brighter plumage, stronger wing: the breeze
Of Alpine heights thou playest with, borne on
Beyond Sorrento and Amalfi, where
The Siren waits thee, singing song for song.

W. S. Landor

13

I know that all beneath the moon decays,
And what by mortals in this world is brought,
In Time's great periods shall return to nought;
That fairest states have fatal nights and days;
I know how all the Muse's heavenly lays,
With toil of spright which are so dearly bought,
As idle sounds, of few or none are sought,
And that nought lighter is than airy praise;
I know frail beauty's like the purple flower,
To which one morn oft birth and death affords;
That love a jarring is of minds' accords,
Where sense and will bring under reason's power.
Know what I list, this all can not me move,
But that, O me! I both must write and love.

William Drummond

14

If all the pens that ever poets held,
Had fed the feeling of their masters' thoughts,
And every sweetness that inspir'd their hearts,
Their minds, and muses on admirèd themes;
If all the heavenly quintessènce they still
From their immortal flowers of poesy,
Wherein, as in a mirror, we perceive
The highest reaches of a human wit;
If these had made one poem's period,

And all combin'd in beauty's worthiness,
Yet should there hover in their restless heads
One thought, one grace, one wonder, at the least,
Which into words no virtue can digest.

Christopher Marlowe

15

Since brass, nor stone, nor earth, nor boundless sea,
But sad mortality o'ersways their power,
How with this rage shall beauty hold a plea,
Whose action is no stronger than a flower?
O! how shall summer's honey breath hold out
Against the wrackful siege of battering days,
When rocks impregnable are not so stout,
Nor gates of steel so strong, but Time decays?
O fearful meditation! where, alack,
Shall Time's best jewel from Time's chest lie hid?
Or what strong hand can hold his swift foot back?
Or who his spoil of beauty can forbid?
  O! none, unless this miracle have might,
  That in black ink my love may still shine bright.

Shakespeare

16

If thou survive my well-contented day,
When that churl Death my bones with dust shall cover,
And shalt by fortune once more re-survey
These poor rude lines of thy deceased lover,

Compare them with the bettering of the time,
And though they be outstripp'd by every pen,
Reserve them for my love, not for their rime,
Exceeded by the height of happier men.
O! then vouchsafe me but this loving thought:
'Had my friend's Muse grown with this growing age,
A dearer birth than this his love had brought,
To march in ranks of better equipage:
  But since he died, and poets better prove,
  Theirs for their style I'll read, his for his love.'

Shakespeare

17

Give all to love;
Obey thy heart;
Friends, kindred, days,
Estate, good-fame,
Plans, credit, and the Muse,—
Nothing refuse.

'Tis a brave master;
Let it have scope:
Follow it utterly,
Hope beyond hope:
High and more high
It dives into noon,
With wing unspent,
Untold intent;

But it is a god,
Knows its own path,
And the outlets of the sky.

It was not for the mean;
It requireth courage stout,
Souls above doubt,
Valour unbending;
Such 'twill reward,—
They shall return
More than they were,
And ever ascending.

Leave all for love;
Yet, hear me, yet,
One word more thy heart behoved,
One pulse more of firm endeavour,—
Keep thee to-day,
To-morrow, forever,
Free as an Arab
Of thy beloved.

Cling with life to the maid;
But when the surprise,
First vague shadow of surmise
Flits across her bosom young
Of a joy apart from thee,
Free be she, fancy-free;
Nor thou detain her vesture's hem,
Nor the palest rose she flung
From her summer diadem.

December

Though thou loved her as thyself,
As a self of purer clay,
Though her parting dims the day,
Stealing grace from all alive;
Heartily know,
When half-gods go,
The gods arrive.

R. W. Emerson

18

Since there's no help, come let us kiss and part,
Nay, I have done, you get no more of me,
And I am glad, yea glad with all my heart,
That thus so cleanly I myself can free;
Shake hands for ever, cancel all our vows,
And when we meet at any time again,
Be it not seen in either of our brows,
That we one jot of former love retain;
Now at the last gasp of love's latest breath,
When his pulse failing, passion speechless lies,
When faith is kneeling by his bed of death,
And innocence is closing up his eyes,
Now if thou would'st, when all have given him
over,
From death to life thou might'st him yet recover.

Michael Drayton

19

Now that we've done our best and worst, and parted,
  I would fill my mind with thoughts that will not rend.
(O heart, I do not dare go empty-hearted)
  I'll think of Love in books, Love without end;
Women with child, content; and old men sleeping;
  And wet strong ploughlands, scarred for certain grain;
And babes that weep, and so forget their weeping;
  And the young heavens, forgetful after rain;
And evening hush, broken by homing wings;
  And Song's nobility, and Wisdom holy,
That live, we dead. I would think of a thousand things,
  Lovely and durable, and taste them slowly,
One after one, like tasting a sweet food.
I have need to busy my heart with quietude.

Rupert Brooke

20

The days are sad, it is the Holytide—
  Drear clouds have hid the crimson of the West,
  And like the wingèd day, Delight hath died
  Within me, and proud passions gone to rest.
  In this dusk hour, before the lamps are lit,
  Through the heart's long long gallery I will go,
  And mark pale Memory's taper fall on it
  Startling strange hues, like firelight on the snow.

The days are sad, it is the Holytide—
  The Winter morn is short, the Night is long,
  So let the lifeless hours be glorified
  With deathless thoughts, and echoed in sweet song;
  And thro' the sunset of this purple cup
  They will resume the roses of their prime,
  And the old Dead will hear us, and wake up,
  Pass with dim smiles, and make our hearts sublime!
The days are sad, it is the Holytide—
  Be dusky mistletoes and hollies strown,
  Sharp as the spear that pierced His sacred side,
  Red as the drops upon His thorny crown;
  No haggard Passion and no lawless Mirth
  Fright off the sombre Muse—tell sweet old tales,
  Sing songs, as we sit bending o'er the hearth,
  Till the lamp flickers, and the memory fails.

Frederick Tennyson

21

  Blow, blow, thou winter wind,
  Thou art not so unkind
    As man's ingratitude;
  Thy tooth is not so keen,
  Because thou art not seen,
    Although thy breath be rude.
Heigh ho! sing, heigh ho! unto the green holly:
Most friendship is feigning, most loving mere folly:
    Then heigh ho, the holly!
    This life is most jolly.

Freeze, freeze, thou bitter sky,
That dost not bite so nigh
    As benefits forgot:
Though thou the waters warp,
Thy sting is not so sharp
    As friend remember'd not.
Heigh ho! sing, heigh ho! unto the green holly:
Most friendship is feigning, most loving mere folly:
    Then heigh ho, the holly;
    This life is most jolly.

Shakespeare

22

Nay, Ivy: nay, it shall not be i-wys;
Let Holy hafe the maystery, as the maner ys.
Holy stond in the Halle, fayre to behold;
Ivy stond without the dore; she is full sore acold.

Holy and hys mery men they dawnsyn and they sing,
Ivy and hur maydenys they wepyn and they wryng.

Ivy hath berys as black as any slo;
Ther com the oule and ete hym as she goo.

Holy hath byrdys, a ful fayre flok,
The nyghtyngale, the poppyngy, the gayntyl lavyrok.

Good Ivy! what byrdys ast thou?
Non but the howlet that kreye ' How! how!'
Nay, Ivy, nay, it shall not be i-wys;
Let Holy hafe the maystery, as the maner ys.

Old Carol

December

23

Come, bring with a noise,
My merrie merrie boyes,
The Christmas Log to the firing;
While my good Dame, she
Bids ye all be free;
And drink to your hearts desiring.

With the last yeeres brand
Light the new block, And
For good successe in his spending,
On your Psaltries play,
That sweet luck may
Come while the Log is a teending.

Drink now the strong Beere,
Cut the white loafe here,
The while the meat is a shredding;
For the rare Mince-Pie
And the Plums stand by
To fill the Paste that's a kneading.

Robert Herrick

24

And well our Christian sires of old
Loved when the year its course had roll'd,
And brought blithe Christmas back again,
With all his hospitable train.
Domestic and religious rite
Gave honour to the holy night;
On Christmas eve the bells were rung;
On Christmas eve the mass was sung:
That only night, in all the year,
Saw the stoled priest the chalice rear.
The damsel donn'd her kirtle sheen;
The hall was dress'd with holly green;
Forth to the wood did merry-men go,
To gather in the mistletoe.
Then open'd wide the Baron's hall
To vassal, tenant, serf, and all;
Power laid his rod of rule aside,
And Ceremony doff'd his pride.
The heir, with roses in his shoes,
That night might village partner choose;
The Lord, underogating, share
The vulgar game of 'post and pair.'
All hail'd, with uncontroll'd delight,
And general voice, the happy night,
That to the cottage, as the crown,
Brought tidings of salvation down.

Scott

25

It was the winter wild,
While the Heaven-born Child
   All meanly wrapt in the rude manger lies;
Nature in awe to him
Had doffed her gaudy trim,
   With her great Master so to sympathize:
It was no season then for her
To wanton with the sun her lusty paramour.

Only with speeches fair
She woos the gentle air
   To hide her guilty front with innocent snow,
And on her naked shame
Pollute with sinful blame,
   The saintly veil of maiden white to throw,
Confounded, that her Maker's eyes
Should look so near upon her foul deformities.

But He her fears to cease,
Sent down the meek-eyed Peace;
   She crown'd with olive green, came softly sliding
Down through the turning sphere,
His ready harbinger,
   With turtle wing the amorous clouds dividing,
And waving wide her myrtle wand,
She strikes a universal peace through sea and land.

No war or battle's sound
Was heard the world around,
   The idle spear and shield were high up-hung;
The hooked chariot stood
Unstained with hostile blood,
   The trumpet spake not to the armed throng,
And kings sate still with awful eye,
As if they surely knew their sovran Lord was by.

But peaceful was the night
Wherein the Prince of Light
   His reign of peace upon the earth began:
The winds with wonder whist,
Smoothly the waters kist,
   Whispering new joys to the mild Ocean,
Who now hath quite forgot to rave,
While birds of calm sit brooding on the charmed wave.

The stars with deep amaze
Stand fixed in steadfast gaze,
   Bending one way their precious influence,
And will not take their flight,
For all the morning light,
   Or Lucifer that often warned them thence;
But in their glimmering orbs did glow,
Until their Lord Himself bespake, and bid them go.

And though the shady gloom
Had given day her room,
   The sun himself withheld his wonted speed,
And hid his head for shame,

As his inferior flame,
  The new-enlightened world no more should need;
He saw a greater Sun appear
Then his bright throne, or burning axle-tree could bear

The shepherds on the lawn,
Or ere the point of dawn,
  Sat simply chatting in a rustic row;
Full little thought they than,
That the mighty Pan
  Was kindly come to live with them below;
Perhaps their loves or else their sheep,
Was all that did their silly thoughts so busy keep.

When such music sweet
Their hearts and ears did greet,
  As never was by mortal finger strook,
Divinely warbled voice
Answering the stringed noise,
  As all their souls in blissful rapture took:
The air such pleasure loth to lose,
With thousand echoes still prolongs each heavenly close.

Nature that heard such sound
Beneath the hollow round
  Of Cynthia's seat, the airy region thrilling,
Now was almost won
To think her part was done,
  And that her reign had here its last fulfilling;
She knew such harmony alone
Could hold all Heaven and Earth in happier union.

At last surrounds their sight
A globe of circular light,
   That with long beams the shame-faced night arrayed,
The helmed cherubim
And sworded seraphim,
   Are seen in glittering ranks with wings displayed,
Harping in loud and solemn quire,
With unexpressive notes to Heaven's new-born Heir.
   .   .   .   .

But see the Virgin blest,
Hath laid her Babe to rest:
   Time is our tedious song should here have ending,
Heaven's youngest teemed star,
Hath fixed her polished car,
   Her sleeping Lord with handmaid lamp attending:
And all about the courtly stable,
Bright-harnessed angels sit in order serviceable.

Milton

26

   Come, we shepherds whose blest sight
      Hath met Love's noon in Nature's night;
      Come, lift we up our loftier song,
   And wake the sun that lies too long.

   We saw Thee in Thy balmy nest,
      Young dawn of our eternal day;
   We saw Thine eyes break from the East,
      And chase the trembling shades away:
   We saw Thee, and we blest the sight,
   We saw Thee by Thine own sweet light.

Poor world, said I, what wilt thou do
   To entertain this starry stranger?
Is this the best thou canst bestow—
   A cold and not too cleanly manger?
Contend, the powers of heaven and earth,
To fit a bed for this huge birth.

Proud world, said I, cease your contest,
   And let the mighty babe alone,
The phoenix builds the phoenix nest,
   Love's architecture is His own.
The babe, whose birth embraves this morn,
Made His own bed ere He was born.

                   Richard Crashaw

27

1*st Shepherd.* Hail, maid-mother, and wife so mild!
   As the angel said, so have we found,
   I have nothing to present with thy child,
   But my pipe; hold, hold! take it in thy hand;
   Wherein much pleasure that I have found,
   And now to honour thy glorious birth,
   Thou shalt it have to make thee mirth.

2*nd Shepherd.* Now, hail be thou, child, and thy dame,
   For in a poor lodging here art thou laid;
   So the angel said, and told us thy name.
   Hold, take thou here my hat on thy head,
   And now of one thing thou art well sped;
   For weather thou hast no need to complain,
   For wind, ne sun, hail, snow, and rain.

3rd Shepherd. Hail, be thou Lord over water and lands
    For thy coming all we may make mirth,
    Have here my mittens to put on thy hands,
    Other treasure have I none to present thee with.

Mary. Now, herdmen hind, for your coming;
    To my child shall I pray,
    As he is heaven king, to grant you his blessing,
    And to his bliss that ye may wynd at your last day.
        (There the Shepherds sing again:)
    Down from heaven, from heaven so high,
    Of angels there came a great company,
    With mirth, and joy, and great solemnity
    They sang, Terli, terlow;
    So merrily the shepherds their pipes can blow.

          (From the Coventry Play of
          the Tailors and Shearmen)

28

1st Prophet. This other night so cold,
    Hereby upon a wold,
    Shepherds watching their fold
    In the night so far,
    To them appeared a star,
    And ever it drew them near,
    Which star they did behold,
    Brighter they say a thousand fold
    Than the sun so clear

In his midday sphere;
And they these tidings told.

2nd Prophet. What, secretly?

1st Prophet. Na, na, hardily,
    They made there of no council,
    For they sang as loud,
    As ever they could,
    Praising the king of Israel.

2nd Prophet. Yet do I marvel,
    In what pile or castle,
    These herdmen did him see.

1st Prophet. Neither in halls, nor yet in bowers,
    Born would he not be,
    Neither in castles, nor yet in towers,
    That seemly were to see,
    But at his Father's will,
    The prophecy to fulfil,
    Betwixt an ox and an ass
    Jesu this king born he was:
    Heaven he bring us till!

2nd Prophet. Sir, ah! but when these shepherds had
        seen him there,
    Into what place did they repair?

1st Prophet. Forth they went, and glad they were;
    Going they did sing,
    With mirth and solace, they made good cheer
    For joy of that new tiding.

And after as I heard they tell
He rewarded them full well.
He granted them heaven therein to dwell.
In are they gone with joy and mirth
And their song it is Noël.

(From the same)

29

'Tis zome vo'ks jaÿ to teäke the road,
An' goo abro'd, a-wand'rèn wide,
Vrom shere to shere, vrom pleäce to pleäce,
The swiftest peäce that vo'k can ride.
But I've a jaÿ 'ithin the door,
Wi' friends avore the vier-zide.

An' zoo, when winter skies do lour,
An' when the Stour's a-rollèn wide,
Drough bridge-voot raïls, a-païnted white,
To be at night the traveller's guide,
Gi'e me a pleäce that's warm an' dry,
A-zittèn nigh my vier-zide.

If, when a friend ha' left the land,
I shook his hand a-most wet-eyed,
I velt too well the op'nèn door
Would leäd noo mwore where he did bide,
An' where I heärd his vaïce's sound,
In me'th around the vier-zide.

December

As I've a-zeed how vast do vall
The mwold'rèn hall, the wold vo'ks pride,
Where merry hearts wer woonce a-ved
Wi' daily bread, why, I've a-sigh'd
To zee the wall so green wi' mwold,
An' vind so cwold the vier-zide.

An' Chris'mas still mid bring his me'th
To ouer he'th, but if we tried
To gather all that woonce did wear
Gay feäces there! Ah! zome ha' died,
An' zome be gone to leäve wi' gaps
O' missèn laps, the vier-zide.

But come now, bring us in your hand
A heavy brand o' woak a-dried,
To cheer us wi' his het an' light,
While vrosty night, so starry-skied,
Do gather souls that time do speäre
To zit an' sheäre our vier-zide.

William Barnes

30

Four Seasons fill the measure of the year;
    There are four seasons in the mind of man:
He has his lusty Spring, when fancy clear
    Takes in all beauty with an easy span:

He has his Summer, when luxuriously
   Spring's honey'd cud of youthful thought he loves
To ruminate, and by such dreaming high
   Is nearest unto heaven: quiet coves
His soul has in its Autumn, when his wings
   He furleth close; contented so to look
On mists in idleness—to let fair things
   Pass by unheeded as a threshold brook.
He has his Winter too of pale misfeature,
Or else he would forego his mortal nature.

                                  Keats

31

For I have learned
To look on nature, not as is the hour
Of thoughtless youth; but hearing oftentimes
The still, sad music of humanity,
Nor harsh nor grating, though of ample power
To chasten and subdue. And I have felt
A presence that disturbs me with the joy
Of elevated thoughts; a sense sublime
Of something far more deeply interfused,
Whose dwelling is the light of setting suns,
And the round ocean and the living air,
And the blue sky, and in the mind of man:
A motion and a spirit, that impels
All thinking things, all objects of all thought,

And rolls through all things. Therefore am I still
A lover of the meadows and the woods,
And mountains; and of all that we behold
From this green earth; of all the mighty world
Of eye, and ear,—both what they half create,
And what perceive; well pleased to recognise
In nature and the language of the sense
The anchor of my purest thoughts, the nurse,
The guide, the guardian of my heart, and soul
Of all my moral being.

Wordsworth

INDEX OF AUTHORS

INDEX OF FIRST LINES